# Telecourse Guide
## for
## Texas Politics and You

Fourth Edition

# Telecourse Guide
## for
## Texas Politics and You

Fourth Edition

NOREEN WARWICK

Revised by John Hitt

Produced by:

Dallas TeleLearning
Dallas County Community College District

THOMSON

WADSWORTH

Australia • Canada • Mexico • Singapore • Spain • United Kingdom • United States

President/LeCroy Center: Pamela K. Quinn
Vice President of Instruction: Jim Picquet
Texas Government Content Specialist: Noreen Warwick
Project Director: Linda Condos
Producer: Pamela Kettle
Producer's Assistant: Nicole Rambo
Instructional Designer: Mary Williams
Research Assistant and Website Development: Linda Camp Keith
Research Assistant and Website Development: Ted Lewis
Senior Instructional Designer: Nora Coto Busby
Marketing Information Specialist: Mary Bills
Telecommunications Information Specialist: Evelyn J. Wong

Telecourse Guide ISBN: 0-534-63131-2
Copyright © 2005 by Dallas County Community College District.

Requests for permission to make copies of any part of the work should be mailed to:
Dallas TeleLearning
9596 Walnut Street
Dallas, Texas 75243

This edition has been printed directly from camera-ready copy.

Printed in the United States of America
1  2  3  4  5  6  7   08  07  06  05  04

Printer: Darby Printing, Inc.

Cover Image: photo courtesy of Texas Department of Transportation

# Contents

# To You, the Student

Our state's government is a vital and constantly changing force in our society that impacts virtually everything we do today and will do in the future.

The telecourse, *Texas Politics and You*, brings the world of Texas government and politics to life through video scenarios of case studies and interviews with government experts.

My goal was to create a course that would be more than an outline of general concepts on Texas politics. I wanted to develop a variety of programs with stimulating conversations integrated with visually supporting information that would give you the opportunity to really learn about concepts by examining actual issues and policies and listening to the people who were and are directly involved. In addition, an analytical approach has been taken; topics are explored through different perspectives to enable you to evaluate and assess issues and outcomes.

You will have the opportunity to experience much of what takes place in the vast state of Texas as you learn about the political process and issues that illustrate federal and state responsibilities, subculture influences on policy making, media influences, the NAFTA impact on Texas, and the real workings of the state and local governments. Successful completion of the telecourse will provide the basis for you to make informed decisions in your role as an active citizen.

—Noreen Warwick
Content Specialist

# Telecourse Organization

*Texas Politics and You* is designed as an integrated learning experience consisting of three elements: telecourse guide, textbook, and video programs.

## TELECOURSE GUIDE

The telecourse guide for this course is:

Warwick, Noreen. *Telecourse Guide for Texas Politics and You.* 4th ed. Belmont, California: West-Wadsworth Publishing Company, 2005. ISBN: 0-534-63131-2.

No course functions effectively without a knowledgeable professor. The professor is an indispensable part of any learning experience, including a telecourse. The telecourse guide directs the student between contacts with the professor. It provides students with assignments; describes textbook objectives, video objectives, and web activities; and provides practice tests. The telecourse guide is the student's pilot or tutor through the course.

Development of the student telecourse guide included work by an instructional design specialist and a content specialist. Each lesson contains a lesson assignment, an overview, a lesson goal, textbook objectives, video objectives, web activities, practice test questions, and answers to provide feedback to the student before formal testing. In addition, names of contributors to this course are listed in the back of the guide. The web activities and practice tests are directly related to lesson objectives. If the telecourse guide recommendations are followed and each lesson video program viewed, all of the requirements for this course should be successfully accomplished.

## TEXTBOOK

In addition to the telecourse guide, a textbook is required for this course:

Text: Kraemer, Richard, et al. *Texas Politics.* 9th ed. Belmont, California: Wadsworth Publishing Company, 2005. ISBN: 0-534-63129-0.

## VIDEO PROGRAMS

The video series for this course is:

*Texas Politics and You.*

The course includes twenty-six video programs, one for each of the twenty-six lessons. Each video program is correlated with the telecourse guide and the lesson assignment. You should read the video objectives in the telecourse guide before you watch the program.

If the programs are broadcast more than once in your area, or if video or audio tapes are available at your college, students might find it helpful to watch the video programs more than once or to listen to an audio tape for review. You are encouraged to record the video programs for subsequent study and review.


## TELECOURSE PLUS

An online interactive option is available to students whose institutions have opted to license the course. The web activities are useful for working with "real-time" information related to the lesson content and objectives. If your course includes this PLUS component, please contact your instructor for the course website address and required password.

# Telecourse Guidelines

Follow these guidelines as you study the material presented in each lesson:

1. LESSON ASSIGNMENTS—
   Review the Lesson Assignments in order to schedule your time appropriately.
   For each lesson, you will have a reading assignment and a video assignment.

2. OVERVIEW—
   The Overview provides a brief narrative introduction describing the lesson focus.

3. LESSON GOAL—
   The Lesson Goal informs students of the information they should have after
   completion of the lesson.

4. TEXTBOOK OBJECTIVES—
   To get the most from your reading, review the Textbook Objectives, then read the
   assignment. You may want to write responses or notes to reinforce what you
   have learned.

5. VIDEO OBJECTIVES—
   To get the most from the video segment of the lesson, review the Video
   Objectives before watching the video. You may want to write responses or notes
   to reinforce what you have learned.

6. WEB RESOURCE PAGE—
   gln.dcccd.edu/txgovernment
   This web resource link is provided for enrichment of the basic course content and
   may be used by your instructor for experiential learning exercises.

7. PRACTICE TEST—
   After reading the assignment, watching the video, and addressing the objectives,
   you should be able to complete the following Practice Test. Some essay
   questions in this Practice Test may be included in your exams. When you have
   completed the Practice Test, turn to the Answer Key to score your answers.

8. ANSWER KEY—
   This Answer Key provides the answers and references for the practice test
   questions. Objectives are referenced using the following abbreviations:
   T=Textbook Objective    V=Video Objective

# Lesson 1

# Texas: Who We Are

## LESSON ASSIGNMENTS

Review the following assignments in order to schedule your time appropriately. For each lesson you will have a reading assignment and a video assignment.

Text:

> Kraemer, et al., *Texas Politics*, Chapter 1, "The Context of Texas Politics," pp. 1–32.

Video:

> "Texas: Who We Are" from the series *Texas Politics and You*.

Activities:

> One or more activities may be assigned to this lesson. Refer to your syllabus.

## OVERVIEW

The history of Texas is summarized in your readings, emphasizing important political events and the development of the economy. Principles of democratic theory are included and are to be used to assess the political system in Texas. You will look at the dynamics of the demographics in Texas and the possible implications such population changes will present to the people of Texas.

## LESSON GOAL

You should be able to analyze current Texas government in the context of its history and assess Texas' ability to cope with population changes and public problems.

# TEXTBOOK OBJECTIVES

The following objectives are designed to help you get the most from the text. Review them before reading the assignment. You may want to write notes to reinforce what you have learned.

1.  Describe the colonization process and events leading to statehood.

2.  Explain how the Civil War and Reconstruction impacted Texas politics then and today.

3.  Describe Texas' historical policy toward business in the nineteenth century.

4.  Explain what the "progressive spirit" means in the early twentieth century.

5.  Explain how World War I events impacted attitudes in Texas.

6.  Describe how the Depression affected Texas and how relief was provided.

7.  Describe how Texas has changed economically since World War II.

8.  Explain the ideals in a democracy, and evaluate how successful Texas has been in achieving these goals.

9.  Assess Texas' political belief system and the record in Texas on spending for state services.

10. Describe important social and economic challenges confronting Texans in the twenty-first century.

# VIDEO OBJECTIVES

The following objectives are designed to help you get the most from the video segment of this lesson. Review them before watching the video. You may want to write notes to reinforce what you have learned.

11. Explain the demographic, economic, and political significance of the expanding minority population in Texas.

12. Explain the challenges of serving the aging population.

13. Assess what Texans must do to have future prosperity and accommodate the new demographic realities.

PRACTICE TEST

After reading the assignment, watching the video, and addressing the objectives, you should be able to complete the following Practice Test. Some essay questions in this Practice Test may be included in your exams. When you have completed the Practice Test, turn to the Answer Key to score your answers.

MULTIPLE CHOICE

Select the single best answer. If more than one answer is required, it will be so indicated.

1. Cultural differences between Mexico and the Anglo settlers in Texas made it difficult for the majority of the settlers to _____
   A. take the oath of allegiance as Mexican citizens.
   B. reject Roman Catholicism.
   C. release black slaves.
   D. accept polygamy.

2. Owners of the railroad entered into agreements to eliminate competition; manufacturing activity continued to grow, and yet, _____
   A. organized labor gained approval by the state to operate under a charter.
   B. labor unions were not accepted in the South as they were elsewhere.
   C. Governor John Ireland used troops to protect the labor strikers.
   D. aggregations of labor called "unions" were protected by the courts in the 1880s and encouraged to operate.

3. The requirement to pay a poll tax as a prerequisite to voting had an especially negative effect on _____
   A. poor Anglos.
   B. Mexican Americans.
   C. African Americans.
   D. Republicans.

4. The growth of the Texas economy in the 1970s was fed in large measure by _____
   A. an increase in federal expenditures in the state.
   B. an increase in the price of oil resulting from the OPEC oil embargo.
   C. an increase in the price of most agricultural commodities.
   D. the shift from a manufacturing to a service economy.

5. What theory of economic and social development holds that if business flourishes, everyone will benefit from the prosperity that follows?
   A. "Hidden hand"
   B. "Golden rule"
   C. "Big brother"
   D. "Trickle-down"

6. By the year 2000, approximately what part of the Texas population was projected to be African American and Hispanic?
   A. Twelve percent
   B. Twenty-two percent
   C. Thirty-two percent
   D. Forty-two percent

7. The influence of the growth of minority groups shows a trend toward _____
   A. an increase in persons who are eligible to vote.
   B. an increase in Latin American representation in state agencies.
   C. total political commitment to incorporating new citizens in the political system.
   D. an increase in Latin American representation at the local level of government.
   E. all but C.

8. The town of Claude, Texas, illustrates the demographic challenge _____
   A. that the minority population brings with diverse language needs.
   B. of providing services for the elderly.
   C. of providing job training skills.
   D. of serving a community that is disproportionately younger.
   E. all of the above.

9. Future prosperity in Texas will require _____
   A. a highly skilled workforce that is increasingly minority.
   B. resources devoted to education.
   C. inclusion of minority representation.
   D. public dialogue to accommodate new realities.
   E. all of the above.

## TRUE/FALSE

If the statement is true, write "T" to the left of the statement. If the statement (or any part of the statement) is false, write "F" to the left of the statement.

10. Because so many Democrats were disqualified from holding political offices as a result of their support for the Confederacy, the Republican party was able to dominate Texas political institutions until well into the twentieth century.

11. In 1922 the Ku Klux Klan's candidate, Earle Mayfield, was elected to the U.S. Senate.

12. The federal government provided for economic relief for the many Texans affected by the Depression.

13. In a democracy, because the people make the laws, they are morally obligated to obey them.

## ESSAY PROBLEM QUESTIONS

14. What impact did the Civil War and Reconstruction have on Texas politics? What aspects of the state's political system continue to show the influence of this period in Texas history?

15. Assess the impact that Texas' conservatism has on the role of government in society toward taxes, education, welfare, and environmental protections.

16. How has Texas changed—politically, socially, and economically—since World War II?

17. Identify and describe the possible implications of the two expanding populations in Texas and what the state must do to meet these challenges.

## ANSWER KEY

The following provides the answers and references for the Practice Test questions. Objectives are referenced using the following abbreviations:

T=Textbook Objectives   V=Video Objectives

| | Answer | Learning Objectives | References |
|---|---|---|---|
| 1. | C | T1 | Kraemer, p. 4 |
| 2. | B | T3 | Kraemer, pp. 8–9 |
| 3. | C | T4 | Kraemer, p. 10 |
| 4. | B | T7 | Kraemer, pp. 14–15 |
| 5. | D | T9 | Kraemer, p. 22 |
| 6. | D | T10 | Kraemer, p. 27 |
| 7. | E | V11 | Video |
| 8. | B | V12 | Video |
| 9. | E | V13 | Video |
| 10. | F | T2 | Kraemer, p. 7 |
| 11. | T | T5 | Kraemer, p. 11 |
| 12. | T | T6 | Kraemer, p. 13 |
| 13. | T | T8 | Kraemer, p. 16 |
| 14. | | T2 | Kraemer, pp. 7–16 |
| 15. | | T9, V11 | Kraemer, pp. 20–26; Video |
| 16. | | T10, V11 | Kraemer, pp. 11–16; Video |
| 17. | | V11, V12, V13 | Video |

# Lesson 2

# The Texas Constitution

## LESSON ASSIGNMENTS

Review the following assignments in order to schedule your time appropriately. For each lesson you will have a reading assignment and a video assignment.

Text:

Kraemer, et al., *Texas Politics*, Chapter 2, "The Constitutional Setting," pp. 34–60.

Video:

"The Texas Constitution" from the series *Texas Politics and You*.

Activities:

One or more activities may be assigned to this lesson. Refer to your syllabus.

## OVERVIEW

This lesson explains the purpose of a constitution and discusses the problems associated with the Texas Constitution. Constitutions give legitimacy to the government and outline fundamental rules governing the use of power. A historical overview of the Texas Constitution is presented with explanations of how the present day constitution operates in the context of its past. You will examine the impact of constitutional provisions regarding special interests, learn how and why amendments are made to the Texas Constitution, and analyze why many people feel that Texas needs to revise its constitution.

# LESSON GOAL

You should be able to describe the purpose of a constitution, assess the Texas Constitution, and discuss the political aspects that accompany the amending process.

# TEXTBOOK OBJECTIVES

The following objectives are designed to help you get the most from the text. Review them before reading the assignment. You may want to write notes to reinforce what you have learned.

1.  Explain the four purposes of a constitution.

2.  Describe the circumstances that prompted Texas to adopt six different constitutions from 1836 to 1876.

3.  Describe the principal features of the Texas Constitution and reasons for its style and structure.

4.  Describe how the Texas Constitution is amended.

5.  Summarize the main criticisms of the Texas Constitution.

6.  Describe recent constitutional reform efforts.

7.  Explain why and how special interests are involved in constitutional politics.

# VIDEO OBJECTIVES

The following objectives are designed to help you get the most from the video segment of this lesson. Review them before watching the video. You may want to write notes to reinforce what you have learned.

8.  Define and explain how the attitudes of the delegates affected the writing of the Texas Constitution of 1876.

9.  Describe how the Texas Constitution is amended.

10. Identify the number of amendments through 1997, and explain why the Texas Constitution has been so frequently amended.

11. Explain the claim that a detailed constitution and amendments serve narrow interests.

12. Describe and evaluate the role and significance of the Texas voter in the amendment process.

13. Explain why some people believe that a new constitution is needed.

## PRACTICE TEST

After reading the assignment, watching the video, and addressing the objectives, you should be able to complete the following Practice Test. Some essay questions in this Practice Test may be included in your exams. When you have completed the Practice Test, turn to the Answer Key to score your answers.

## MULTIPLE CHOICE

Select the single best answer. If more than one answer is required, it will be so indicated.

1. When a government's acts are accepted by the citizens as lawful, fair, and just, the government is said to have _____
   A. sovereignty.
   B. authority.
   C. legitimacy.
   D. justice.
   E. all of the above.

2.  What was Texas' most progressive constitution in terms of power and organization?
    A.  The Constitution of the Republic of Texas
    B.  The "Statehood Constitution" of 1845
    C.  The Civil War Constitution of 1861
    D.  The Constitution of 1869
    E.  The Constitution of 1867

3.  The twenty counties that voted against ratification of the Constitution in 1876 were _____
    A.  located in West Texas.
    B.  located in South Texas.
    C.  rural.
    D.  urban.
    E.  divided between rural and urban areas.

4.  The Texas Constitution provides for each of the following EXCEPT _____
    A.  limits on the duration of legislative sessions.
    B.  annual regular sessions of the state legislature.
    C.  the popular election of state judges.
    D.  freedom of the press.
    E.  freedom of religion.

5.  Local governments that are governed by a commission combining executive and legislative authority and headed by a judge are _____
    A.  counties.
    B.  municipalities.
    C.  general-law cities.
    D.  special districts.
    E.  school districts.

6.  Amendments to the Texas Constitution may be proposed by _____
    A.  the legislature only.
    B.  either the legislature or the governor.
    C.  either the legislature or the state's voters.
    D.  either the governor or the state's voters.
    E.  none of the above.

7. Amendments to the Texas Constitution are proposed by the legislature and are ratified by _____
   A. a three-fourths vote of the membership of the Supreme Court of Texas.
   B. a two-thirds vote of the Court of Criminal Appeals.
   C. the governor.
   D. a majority of the voters in a general election or special election called to ratify amendments to the Texas Constitution.

8. Over the last century, most amendments to the Texas Constitution have dealt with policy issues that many say should have been resolved by the _____
   A. executive branch.
   B. legislature.
   C. state courts.
   D. Congress.

9. Those who criticize the Texas Constitution believe that ideally, a constitution should be _____
   A. written in general language.
   B. similar to statutory law.
   C. very detailed.
   D. able to solve specific policy problems.

10. Which of the following is not part of the proposed new constitution drafted by Sen. John Montford in 1991?
    A. Term limits for state legislators
    B. Term limits for the governor and lieutenant governor
    C. Nonpartisan elections for state judges
    D. Ordinance power for counties, subject to local voter approval
    E. Elimination of the Permanent University Fund (PUF)

11. Special interests in Texas often attempt to have policies favoring them included in the constitution because _____
    A. there is great prestige in having their "own" provisions in the constitution.
    B. the constitution is more difficult to change than ordinary laws.
    C. constitutional amendments can be approved more quickly than ordinary laws.
    D. voters tend to pay little attention to what is done to the constitution.
    E. all of the above.

12. The Reconstruction Republicans in Texas _____
    A. were the majority in the delegation selected to write the Texas Constitution of 1876.
    B. favored a limited government.
    C. created centralized authority.
    D. operated governmental programs with little expense passed on to the people.

13. Amendments to the Texas Constitution are ratified when they receive approval by _____
    A. the governor.
    B. the Speaker of the House.
    C. the lieutenant governor.
    D. a simple majority of the popular vote on the amendment.

14. The Texas Constitution has grown with amendments because _____
    A. the constitution was written in such a restrictive manner that the state needed constitutional authority to respond to economic changes.
    B. legislators did not have the flexibility to respond to changing needs.
    C. interest groups who benefit from the amendment are actively involved.
    D. all of the above.

15. Once a provision becomes a part of the constitution _____
    A. it is more difficult to change.
    B. it gives the beneficiaries an advantage.
    C. it can be amended.
    D. all of the above.

16. Reasons that are given when proposed amendments are rejected include
_____

    A. confusing language and ignorance of the issue.

    B. tax increases would result in passage.

    C. strong opposition.

    D. all of the above.

17. Many state leaders have called for a new Texas Constitution because they claim that _____

    A. the existing document is too cumbersome.

    B. the governor does not have adequate power.

    C. lawmakers need more flexibility in the constitution to respond to societal needs.

    D. all of the above.

## TRUE/FALSE

If the statement is true, write "T" to the left of the statement. If the statement (or any part of the statement) is false, write "F" to the left of the statement.

18. Both the Texas Constitution and the U.S. Constitution are based on the principle of separation of powers.

19. Because they feared the possible abuse of power by the government, the framers of the Texas Constitution refused to include any checks and balances in the document.

## ESSAY PROBLEM QUESTIONS

20. What were the circumstances that prompted Texas to adopt six different constitutions from 1836 to 1876? In what ways do these constitutions reflect the circumstances surrounding their preparation?

21. How is the Texas Constitution amended? What accounts for the fact that it has been amended 390 times (through 2000) while the U.S. Constitution has been amended only twenty seven times? Evaluate the role of the voter.

22. Explain and assess the reasons the experts give for wanting to revise the Texas Constitution. Discuss and evaluate the views of Senator Ratliff and former Senator Montfort.

23. Explain why policy changes are often made by amending the state constitution rather than by legislation. Give examples of two interest groups that benefit from having their issues addressed in the constitution and explain why this occurs.

## ANSWER KEY

The following provides the answers and references for the Practice Test questions. Objectives are referenced using the following abbreviations:

T=Textbook Objectives   V=Video Objectives

| | Answer | Learning Objectives | References |
|---|---|---|---|
| 1. | C | T1 | Kraemer, p. 35 |
| 2. | D | T2 | Kraemer, p. 39 |
| 3. | D | T3 | Kraemer, p. 40 |
| 4. | B | T3 | Kraemer, pp. 42–46 |
| 5. | A | T3 | Kraemer, p. 47 |
| 6. | A | T4 | Kraemer, p. 48 |
| 7. | D | T4 | Kraemer, p. 48 |
| 8. | B | T4 | Kraemer, p. 51 |
| 9. | A | T5 | Kraemer, p. 51 |
| 10. | E | T6 | Kraemer, p. 53 |
| 11. | B | T7 | Kraemer, p. 56 |
| 12. | C | V8 | Video |
| 13. | D | V9 | Video |
| 14. | D | V10 | Video |
| 15. | D | V11 | Video |
| 16. | D | V12 | Video |
| 17. | D | V13 | Video |
| 18. | T | T3 | Kraemer, p. 43 |
| 19. | F | T3 | Kraemer, p. 43 |
| 20. | | T2 | Kraemer, pp. 37–39 |
| 21. | | T4 | Kraemer, pp. 48–51 |
| 22. | | T5 | Kraemer, pp. 48–55 |
| 23. | | V10, V11 | Video |

# Lesson 3

# The Politics of the Environment

## LESSON ASSIGNMENTS

Review the following assignments in order to schedule your time appropriately. For each lesson you will have a reading assignment and a video assignment.

Text:

Kraemer, et al., *Texas Politics*, Chapter 14, "Issues in Public Policy," pp. 433–442.

Video:

"The Politics of the Environment" from the series *Texas Politics and You*.

Activities:

One or more activities may be assigned to this lesson. Refer to your syllabus.

## OVERVIEW

Texas has many needs to address as it struggles to keep up with the demands that it is facing as it proceeds into the twenty-first century. The programs and services that elected officials provide for the public reflect an effort to establish priorities within the confines of a limited budget. Industry sources maintain that costs of improvements to existing facilities to provide cleaner air and cleaner water are astronomical and would cause many workers to lose jobs. Environmentalists assert that industry must stop polluting its air and water whatever the cost. One enormous challenge is to clean and protect the environment and at the same time, not suppress the economy with excessive regulations.

# LESSON GOAL

Identify and assess the environmental problems and solutions facing Texas, and discuss the political forces that are involved in addressing these problems.

# TEXTBOOK OBJECTIVES

The following objectives are designed to help you get the most from the text. Review them before reading the assignment. You may want to write notes to reinforce what you have learned.

1. Describe how potential public policy makes its way onto the policy agenda for the state.

2. Explain why environmental issues are particularly important to Texans.

3. Describe three basic kinds of water problems in Texas.

4. Explain how national, state, and local governments help shape the environmental public policy agenda of Texas.

5. Assess the quality of air in Texas.

6. Describe the problems of solid waste disposal, and assess the four possible solutions.

7. Explain why the state has had a history of addressing environmental problems in piecemeal fashion.

# VIDEO OBJECTIVES

The following objectives are designed to help you get the most from the video segment of this lesson. Review them before watching the video. You may want to write notes to reinforce what you have learned.

8. Explain the mission and procedures of the Texas Natural Resource Conservation Commission (TNRCC), and evaluate the opportunities for citizen participation.

9. Identify the concerns in the city of Midlothian, Texas, and assess the impact that individuals can have on environmental policies and quality-of-life issues in their communities.

10. Explain the goals of Texans for a sound economy.

11. Define and identify *colonias* in Texas, and discuss the process involved in the Small Town Environmental Project (STEP).

12. Explain the economic and environmental concerns involving the Pantex plant in Amarillo, and identify avenues for citizen participation.

## PRACTICE TEST

After reading the assignment, watching the video, and addressing the objectives, you should be able to complete the following Practice Test. Some essay questions in this Practice Test may be included in your exams. When you have completed the Practice Test, turn to the Answer Key to score your answers.

MULTIPLE CHOICE

Select the single best answer. If more than one answer is required, it will be so indicated.

1. Setting the policy agenda in Texas involves _____
   A. efforts of the governor and key legislators.
   B. interest groups expressing preferences.
   C. federal mandates.
   D. all of the above.
   E. none of the above.

2. The Clean Water Act and the Clean Air Act of 1996 _____
   A. are examples of the high standards that are set by Texas lawmakers.
   B. are national laws that Texas surpasses.
   C. are national laws with standards Texas has had problems in meeting.
   D. were created by the business lobby.

3. The national government _____
   A. has mandated a cleanup of the environment.
   B. has included standards that are expensive to implement.
   C. has not provided adequate funding to assist state and local governments in meeting the standards.
   D. all of the above.

4. The water problem that was the focus of most policy discussion prior to the 1990s was _____
   A. water supply.
   B. water quality.
   C. water damage.
   D. none of the above.

5. The 1995 Texas legislature was identified as "one of the least environmentally sensitive" because it _____
   A. instituted a statewide auto emissions testing program.
   B. dismantled the state's auto emissions testing program.
   C. limited the use of high-sulfur coal in power plants.
   D. mandated the use of natural gas-powered automobiles by state agencies.

6. Texas has been cited as the nation's number one air polluter because _____
   A. of large volumes of auto emissions.
   B. of where it is located geographically.
   C. of acid rain.
   D. it is the second-largest state.

7. Environmental policy making _____
   A. tends to produce diametrically opposed views and make compromise difficult.
   B. has been addressed in piecemeal fashion in Texas.
   C. has faced opposition from many urban counties.
   D. all of the above.

8.  In Texas, citizens who are concerned about businesses that engage in practices that may be detrimental to the environment _____
    A.  may attend and listen to public hearings held by the Texas Natural Resource Conservation Commission.
    B.  may testify and participate in public hearings held by the Texas Natural Resource Conservation Commission.
    C.  may attend open hearings and be appointed an attorney by the state.
    D.  A and B only.

9.  Concerned citizens formed a grassroots organization called Downwinders at Risk and launched 1,400 balloons _____
    A.  to show the number of members and thus their potential strength.
    B.  to celebrate the prosecution of 1,400 polluters.
    C.  to stop the airplanes that were engaging in noise pollution.
    D.  to illustrate how far wind travels and how far pollution can be carried.

10. According to Peggy Venable, from Texans for a Sound Economy, governmental regulations _____
    A.  are costly to business entities.
    B.  are costly to consumers.
    C.  need to be balanced with the need for jobs and a sound economy.
    D.  all of the above.

11. The purpose of the Small Town Environmental Project is to _____
    A.  involve the community of residents, private agencies, and government in resolving environmental problems.
    B.  target small areas for disposal of nuclear waste.
    C.  go around the state and recruit members into the Sierra Club.
    D.  all of the above.

12. The Panhandle Area Neighbors and Landowners and Serious Texans Against Nuclear Dumping (STAND) _____

    A. are proponents of the expansion of the Pantex plant because it provides for more jobs in their community.
    B. have researched other countries where similar work has been done and have found that the entire economy benefits.
    C. resist the expansion of the Pantex plant because of the increase in the population of the area.
    D. resist the expansion of the Pantex plant because of the potential risks to groundwater.

## TRUE/FALSE

If the statement is true, write "T" to the left of the statement. If the statement (or any part of the statement) is false, write "F" to the left of the statement.

13. Regulations on environmental protection and land development are uniform throughout the state of Texas.

## ESSAY PROBLEM QUESTIONS

14. How have federal laws shaped environmental policy in Texas? Do you think the problems addressed in these requirements from the federal government would eventually be solved by the state without pressure from the federal government? Why or why not?

15. Explain the challenges facing the future of Texas' environment, and assess whether the government is doing too little or too much.

16. Identify and evaluate the political forces that are involved in making environmental policy.

17. Refer to the video and assess the impact individuals can have on environmental policies and quality-of-life issues in their communities.

# ANSWER KEY

The following provides the answers and references for the Practice Test questions. Objectives are referenced using the following abbreviations:

T=Textbook Objectives   V=Video Objectives

| | Answer | Learning Objectives | References |
|---|---|---|---|
| 1. | D | T1 | Kraemer, pp. 433–434 |
| 2. | C | T1 | Kraemer, pp. 433–434 |
| 3. | D | T2 | Kraemer, p. 433 |
| 4. | A | T3 | Kraemer, p. 434 |
| 5. | B | T5 | Kraemer, p. 436 |
| 6. | A | T5 | Kraemer, p. 436 |
| 7. | D | T7 | Kraemer, p. 439 |
| 8. | A | V8 | Video |
| 9. | D | V9 | Video |
| 10. | D | V10 | Video |
| 11. | A | V11 | Video |
| 12. | D | V12 | Video |
| 13. | F | T4 | Kraemer, p. 439 |
| 14. | | T1, T4, V8–V12 | Kraemer, pp. 433–440; Video |
| 15. | | T1, T4, T7, V8–V12 | Kraemer, pp. 433–442; Video |
| 16. | | T1, V8–V12 | Kraemer, pp. 433–442; Video |
| 17. | | T1, T2, V8–V12 | Kraemer, pp. 433–442 Video |

# Lesson 4

# Federalism and Texas

## LESSON ASSIGNMENTS

Review the following assignments in order to schedule your time appropriately.
For each lesson you will have a reading assignment and a video assignment.

Text:

> Kraemer, et al., *Texas Politics*, Chapter 1, "Texas and American
> Federalism," pp. 17–18 and Chapter 8, "The Governor," pp. 225–226.

Video:

> "Federalism and Texas" from the series *Texas Politics and You.*

Activities:

> One or more activities may be assigned to this lesson. Refer to your
> syllabus.

## OVERVIEW

One of the goals at the U.S. Constitutional Convention was to create a strong
national government yet permit the states to continue with their major
responsibilities. Federalism was the solution. The United States has a federal
system of government where power is divided between a central government and
the state governments. The U.S. Constitution allocates the power between the
state and national governments and also limits the power of both. However, the
U.S. Constitution does not clearly specify the responsibilities of each. Through
constitutional amendments and court interpretations, the power of the national
government has grown.

The history of federalism reflects changes in attitude about the power and
responsibilities of national and state governments. In the 1980s, the federal
government under President Reagan's leadership sought a reduction in the scope
of federal activities. Fiscal constraints in the 1990s furthered the move to

withdraw financial support, thus leaving the states to serve as "laboratories" to work out their own solutions to policy problems. Though the national government's powers have expanded, the states remain as important participants representing local and diverse interests in this complex system of relationships.

## LESSON GOAL

Explain how the government and politics of Texas are affected by the federal system.

## TEXTBOOK OBJECTIVE

The following objective is designed to help you get the most from the text. Review it before reading the assignment. You may want to write notes to reinforce what you have learned.

1. Identify seven areas where the federal government has an impact on Texas government.

## VIDEO OBJECTIVES

The following objectives are designed to help you get the most from the video segment of this lesson. Review them before watching the video. You may want to write notes to reinforce what you have learned.

2. Explain how federalism reflects a changing attitude about the power and responsibilities of the national and state governments.

3. Explain and assess how representation in Congress impacts Texas.

4. Explain how the "renaissance program" is an example of a federal-local partnership.

5. Explain how the child support program in Texas is an example of a federal-state partnership, and discuss the advantages and disadvantages of federalizing this program.

6. Discuss devolution and the advantages and disadvantages of shifting more of the responsibilities back to the states.

## PRACTICE TEST

After reading the assignment, watching the video, and addressing the objectives, you should be able to complete the following Practice Test. Some essay questions in this Practice Test may be included in your exams. When you have completed the Practice Test, turn to the Answer Key to score your answers.

MULTIPLE CHOICE

Select the single best answer. If more than one answer is required, it will be so indicated.

1. The economy and policies of the state are affected by _____
   A. federal grants.
   B. the location of veterans hospitals and military bases.
   C. federal mandates requiring public buildings to meet requirements making buildings accessible to physically impaired people.
   D. all of the above.
   E. none of the above.

2. Federalism reflects how power and responsibility _____
   A. are permanently allocated between the national and state governments.
   B. change and shift between the national and state governments.
   C. are permanently allocated to the states.
   D. are permanently allocated to the national government.

3. Texans in Congress _____
   A. constantly work to influence national policies and legislation in ways that will benefit the people back home.
   B. have impressive influence because they have a large delegation.
   C. lobbied hard to bring the National Aeronautics and Space Administration's mission control center and astronaut training facility to Texas.
   D. all of the above.

4. Ms. Marshall's neighborhood experienced a "renaissance" as a result of _____
   A. the Texas Healthy Kids Corporation.
   B. a community development block grant program.
   C. a $25 million federal loan.
   D. both B and C.

5. The state program to collect child support has been _____
   A. entirely funded by the federal government.
   B. updated with federal matching grants.
   C. totally opposed to federal help.
   D. terminated and replaced with a national program.

6. The concept of devolution is consistent with the belief that _____
   A. centralized policies are more efficient.
   B. states should be free to work out solutions to their own problems.
   C. the national government has greater resources and should help states and local governments with their problems.
   D. the national government should raise taxes.

7. An example of a state solution to assisting children with health coverage is the _____
   A. Texas Healthy Kids Corporation.
   B. Texas Renaissance Program.
   C. Texas Office of State and Federal Relations.
   D. Texas State Insurance Program.

ESSAY PROBLEM QUESTIONS

8. Explain and give two examples of how the government and politics of Texas are affected by the federal system.

9. Assess the method of collecting child support in Texas, and decide whether this is a program that should be kept in the states or federalized.

10. Explain how the initiative taken by Texas to meet the needs of the growing number of uninsured children is an example of the innovative potential of federalism.

## ANSWER KEY

The following provides the answers and references for the Practice Test questions. Objectives are referenced using the following abbreviations:

T=Textbook Objectives   V=Video Objectives

| | Answer | Learning Objectives | References |
|---|---|---|---|
| 1. | D | T1 | Kraemer, pp. 17–18 |
| 2. | B | V 2 | Video |
| 3. | D | V 3 | Video |
| 4. | D | V 4 | Video |
| 5. | B | V 5 | Video |
| 6. | B | V 6 | Video |
| 7. | A | V 6 | Video |
| 8. | | V2, V3, V4, V5, V6 | Video |
| 9. | | V 5 | Video |
| 10. | | V 6 | Video |

# Lesson 5

## Local Governments in Texas

### LESSON ASSIGNMENTS

Review the following assignments in order to schedule your time appropriately. For each lesson you will have a reading assignment and a video assignment.

Text:

Kraemer, et al., *Texas Politics*, Chapter 12, "Local Government," pp. 343–380.

Video:

"Local Governments in Texas" from the series *Texas Politics and You*.

Activities:

One or more activities may be assigned to this lesson. Refer to your syllabus.

### OVERVIEW

Local government is the government closest to the people and includes counties, cities, and special districts. Local government affects our daily lives much more than state and national governments and provides many opportunities for individual involvement. Texas cities and counties face financial problems due to increases in population and escalating demands for physical improvement and other quality-of-life concerns including police and fire protection and ways to address poverty, racial conflict, and housing. Depending on the political leadership, financial resources, and public support, various solutions to domestic problems are being devised and implemented.

## LESSON GOAL

Identify the different types of local governments (counties, cities, special districts, councils of governments [COGs]), and analyze their major functions as they address important issues.

## TEXTBOOK OBJECTIVES

The following objectives are designed to help you get the most from the text. Review them before reading the assignment. You may want to write notes to reinforce what you have learned.

1. Describe the purpose and creation of Texas county government, and assess the impact of its discretionary authority.

2. Explain why the county commissioner's court is the primary executive and legislative body for the county in Texas.

3. Describe the responsibilities of the county judge, sheriff, county clerk, and justices of the peace.

4. Outline the different sources of revenue for county government, and account for the variation in expenditures among different counties.

5. Evaluate the positive and negative aspects of county government, and assess the likelihood of reform.

6. Explain the difference between general-law and home-rule cities.

7. Describe how extraterritorial jurisdiction and annexation helps Texas cities deal with urban problems.

8. Describe the different characteristics of the basic forms of city government in Texas.

9. Identify the major financial problems for city government.

10. Evaluate the various electoral systems used in Texas cities.

11. Explain why a special district is classified as a government, and assess the advantages and disadvantages.

12. Identify and assess the role of councils of governments (COGs).

13. Explain where and how to participate in local government.

## VIDEO OBJECTIVES

The following objectives are designed to help you get the most from the video segment of this lesson. Review them before watching the video. You may want to write notes to reinforce what you have learned.

14. Describe the factors that prompt some families to move to the suburbs and others to live in the city.

15. Explain how competition between local governments is a problem that Dallas and other large Texas cities face today.

16. Explain why the Brimer Bill and the development of a downtown sports arena were important to Dallas Mayor Ron Kirk.

17. Assess the role of the Citizens Council.

18. Discuss Dallas Area Rapid Transit (DART) and the Trinity River Project, and explain how special districts and the North Texas Council of Governments help local governments work together to solve common problems.

# PRACTICE TEST

After reading the assignment, watching the video, and addressing the objectives, you should be able to complete the following Practice Test. Some essay questions in this Practice Test may be included in your exams. When you have completed the Practice Test, turn to the Answer Key to score your answers.

## MULTIPLE CHOICE

Select the single best answer. If more than one answer is required, it will be so indicated.

1. Except in the few counties using a unit system, the construction and maintenance of county roads and bridges is the responsibility of _____
   A. the county judge.
   B. individual county commissioners.
   C. the assessor-collector of taxes.
   D. the county engineer.
   E. none of the above.

2. Which of the following officials presides over the county commissioners' court?
   A. County judge
   B. County clerk
   C. County attorney
   D. County tax assessor-collector
   E. Sheriff

3. The largest single source of income for the county in Texas is the _____
   A. sales tax.
   B. individual income tax.
   C. corporate income tax.
   D. property tax.
   E. gasoline tax.

4.  Expenditures facing densely populated urban counties include _____
    A.  highways and transportation.
    B.  hospitals, health, and welfare.
    C.  jails.
    D.  all of the above.

5.  Cities in Texas may choose to form their own city charters if they have a population over _____
    A.  1,000.
    B.  5,000.
    C.  10,000.
    D.  20,000.
    E.  50,000.

6.  Except for Houston and El Paso, Texas' largest cities all operate with which form of city government?
    A.  Strong mayor-council
    B.  Weak mayor-council
    C.  Commission
    D.  Commission-manager
    E.  Council-manager

7.  The Texas 8-percent rollback law limits the ability of municipal governments to raise _____
    A.  income taxes.
    B.  sales taxes.
    C.  property taxes.
    D.  ad valorem taxes.
    E.  user fees.

8.  Special districts have the advantage of _____
    A.  being easy to establish and operate.
    B.  offering great flexibility to governmental organizations.
    C.  being able to remove technical problems from the political arena.
    D.  bypassing the legal and organizational limitations of existing governments.
    E.  all of the above.

9. Councils of governments (COGs) function as _____
   A. planning and coordinating bodies for local governments.
   B. state "watchdogs" to monitor local governments.
   C. federal "watchdogs" to monitor local governments.
   D. policy making boards for special districts.
   E. none of the above.

10. Families who choose to live in the city do so because _____
    A. they find it appealing.
    B. they work there.
    C. they like diversity and action.
    D. all of the above.

11. Generally, when businesses relocate to outlying areas away from the urban center _____
    A. the tax base shrinks.
    B. important services to the whole area become more difficult to fund.
    C. museums and symphonies prosper and more get built.
    D. A and B only.

12. The Brimer Bill was important to the city of Dallas because _____
    A. it allows a city to obtain additional revenue to fund arenas and other major public works facilities.
    B. it allowed the city to evict the Dr. Pepper plant.
    C. it will fund the development of the Trinity River Project.
    D. all of the above.

13. The Citizens Council in Dallas _____
    A. is a business organization that has recently taken on the mission of improving the impoverished inner city.
    B. is a women's organization that has recently focused on working with neighborhood gangs.
    C. is a business organization that has recently purchased tracts in the inner city and has displaced many minorities.
    D. is a governmental organization responsible for job training of inner-city youth.

14. Rapid transit service in Dallas is supported by _____
    A. private donations.
    B. a one-cent sales tax levied by a special district.
    C. fares.
    D. both B and C.

15. The North Texas Council of Governments is involved with the Trinity River Project because _____
    A. it is charged by the legislature with looking at long-term development for its region.
    B. it is legally responsible for the river.
    C. it is legally responsible for flood control.
    D. it has the responsibility for taxing and passing legislation.

TRUE/FALSE

If the statement is true, write "T" to the left of the statement. If the statement (or any part of the statement) is false, write "F" to the left of the statement.

16. Because county officials are responsible for administering state laws and programs, they are carefully supervised by state officials.

17. Acting through such interest groups as the Texas Association of County Officials (TACO), county government officials have pushed hard for constitutional changes in the structure and function of county government.

18. Annexation has been used by Texas cities as a means of avoiding the erosion of the tax base caused by the migration of the middle class to the suburbs.

19. All city council elections in Texas are partisan and involve either at-large or place systems.

## ESSAY PROBLEM QUESTIONS

20. In what ways do counties serve as the agents of state government in Texas? What are some of the factors that tend to impede the ability of the state government to supervise the counties? What constitutional changes would you recommend to make counties more accountable to the state or, conversely, more responsive to local problems?

21. What are the advantages and disadvantages of each of the basic types of city government discussed in the text? Why has the council-manager form become the most popular type of city government in Texas' home-rule cities?

22. Why are special districts increasing in number more rapidly than other forms of local government? Do special districts tend to increase or decrease the degree of control that citizens are able to exercise over public policy?

23. Explain five ways to participate in local government.

24. Assess what the city of Dallas, Texas, has done to create a thriving environment for businesses, families, and the development of its lower income areas.

# ANSWER KEY

The following provides the answers and references for the Practice Test questions. Objectives are referenced using the following abbreviations:

T=Textbook Objectives   V=Video Objectives

| | Answer | Learning Objectives | References |
|---|---|---|---|
| 1. | B | T2 | Kraemer, p. 344 and p. 347 |
| 2. | A | T3 | Kraemer, p. 347 |
| 3. | D | T4 | Kraemer, p. 350 |
| 4. | D | T4 | Kraemer, p. 350 |
| 5. | B | T6 | Kraemer, p. 356 |
| 6. | E | T8 | Kraemer, p. 359 |
| 7. | C | T9 | Kraemer, p. 365 |
| 8. | E | T11 | Kraemer, pp. 371–374 |
| 9. | A | T12 | Kraemer, p. 377 |
| 10. | D | V 14 | Video |
| 11. | D | V 15 | Video |
| 12. | A | V 16 | Video |
| 13. | A | V 17 | Video |
| 14. | D | V 18 | Video |
| 15. | A | V 18 | Video |
| 16. | F | T1 | Kraemer, p. 347 |
| 17. | F | T5 | Kraemer, p. 356 |
| 18. | T | T7 | Kraemer, pp. 357–358 |
| 19. | F | T10 | Kraemer, p. 368 |
| 20. | | T1 | Kraemer, pp. 344–356 |
| 21. | | T8 | Kraemer, pp. 356–364 |
| 22. | | T11 | Kraemer, pp. 371–377 |
| 23. | | T13 | Kraemer, p. 378 |
| 24. | | V16, V17, V18 | Video |

# Lesson 6

# Political Culture

## LESSON ASSIGNMENTS

Review the following assignments in order to schedule your time appropriately. For each lesson you will have a reading assignment and a video assignment.

Text:
> Kraemer, et al., *Texas Politics*, Chapter 1, "The Context of Texas Politics," pp. 21–25 and Chapter 4, "Political Parties," pp. 88–95.

Video:
> "Political Culture" from the series *Texas Politics and You.*

Activities:
> One or more activities may be assigned to this lesson. Refer to your syllabus.

## OVERVIEW

The political culture in Texas is one that has embraced the values of traditionalism and individualism favoring elite participation and control. Minorities were basically excluded from the political process. The long history of one dominant conservative party, limited social services, and limited governmental regulations on the environment and businesses reflects these values. But the political culture is changing and varies within the state with growing numbers of its population having different values affecting the nature of policy demands.

## LESSON GOAL

You should be able to describe the subcultures in Texas and explain the political socialization process of how Texans get their opinions and how this affects politics and public policy.

## TEXTBOOK OBJECTIVES

The following objectives are designed to help you get the most from the text. Review them before reading the assignment. You may want to write notes to reinforce what you have learned.

1. Define *political culture*, and explain why the Texas political culture has been distinctive.

2. Contrast *laissez-faire* and *pseudo laissez-faire*, and explain the relationship to social Darwinism.

3. Explain how attitudes and habits of behavior have shaped the politics of Texas.

4. Contrast the two dominant systems of beliefs and values in American and Texas life today.

5. Describe how political attitudes and opinions are formed through the process of political socialization.


## VIDEO OBJECTIVES

The following objectives are designed to help you get the most from the video segment of this lesson. Review them before watching the video. You may want to write notes to reinforce what you have learned.

6. Explain three components of a political culture, and define the role of political socialization.

7. Define the three dominant subcultures classified by Elazar, and use these categories to identify regional differences in Texas.

PRACTICE TEST

After reading the assignment, watching the video, and addressing the objectives, you should be able to complete the following Practice Test. Some essay questions in this Practice Test may be included in your exams. When you have completed the Practice Test, turn to the Answer Key to score your answers.

MULTIPLE CHOICE

Select the single best answer. If more than one answer is required, it will be so indicated.

1. Texas has a well-earned reputation for uniqueness due to _____
   A. the intense state patriotism of Texans.
   B. its experience with slavery.
   C. its defeat in the Civil War.
   D. its extraordinary concern for the general welfare of all people.

2. Consistent with pseudo laissez-faire thinking is _____
   A. antipatriotism.
   B. social Darwinism.
   C. maximum government involvement in economic affairs.
   D. all of the above.

3. The fact that business leaders in Texas often look to government for assistance on their behalf is seen as _____
   A. conservativism.
   B. laissez-faire.
   C. pseudo laissez-faire.
   D. moralistic.

4. Texas has a political culture that is best described as _____
   A. traditionalistic-individualistic.
   B. traditionalistic-moralistic.
   C. individualistic-traditionalistic.
   D. individualistic-moralistic.
   E. moralistic-traditionalistic.

5.  The two dominant ideologies in Texas today are usually referred to as _____
    A.  "individualism" and "communitarianism."
    B.  "socialism" and "populism."
    C.  "libertarianism" and "conservatism."
    D.  "liberalism" and "conservatism."
    E.  none of the above.

6.  In economic policy, the basic principle underlying conservatism is _____
    A.  economic laissez-faire.
    B.  government regulation.
    C.  central planning.
    D.  social equality.
    E.  personal individualism.

7.  Which of the following would be helpful in identifying a political culture?
    A.  The attitudes people hold regarding what government should do
    B.  The attitudes people hold regarding who should rule
    C.  The attitudes people hold regarding what role citizens should play
    D.  All of the above

8.  The acquiring of political values and beliefs from family and institutions is through a process called _____
    A.  majority opinion.
    B.  political socialization.
    C.  social efficacy.
    D.  fostering ideology.

9.  Individuals who are from different regions of the country or within a state will likely have different political values.  This illustrates the existence of a variety of different political _____
    A.  straw polls.
    B.  subcultures.
    C.  campaigns.
    D.  parties.

10. The traditionalistic culture _____
    A. wants experienced politicians running the government.
    B. feels that the national government should do more to help the disadvantaged.
    C. believes that businesses and individuals should let more things be done by government.
    D. stresses that everyone should have an equal opportunity to participate in government.

11. The individualistic culture in Texas is most prominent in _____
    A. East Texas.
    B. the Hill Country.
    C. industrialized cities.
    D. the Gulf Coast region.


TRUE/FALSE

If the statement is true, write "T" to the left of the statement. If the statement (or any part of the statement) is false, write "F" to the left of the statement.

12. Liberals generally support government involvement in both the public and private spheres.


ESSAY PROBLEM QUESTIONS

13. What events in Texas have contributed to the development of the state's political culture? How is Texas changing—politically, socially, and economically? How do these changes affect the state's political culture? Is Texas becoming less distinctive?

14. What are the dominant traits of the traditionalistic political culture? Explain how these traits are manifested in Texas.

15. Explain how to tell a liberal from a conservative.

16. Describe the basic agents of socialization, and explain how these sources of learning affect different people in different ways.

17. Define and explain the three subcultures that are identifiable in Texas, and analyze your political values as you relate to these subculture categories.

## ANSWER KEY

The following provides the answers and references for the Practice Test questions. Objectives are referenced using the following abbreviations:

T=Textbook Objectives   V=Video Objectives

| | Answer | Learning Objectives | References |
|---|---|---|---|
| 1. | A | T1 | Kraemer, p. 22 |
| 2. | B | T2 | Kraemer, p. 23 |
| 3. | C | T2 | Kraemer, p. 23 |
| 4. | A | V6 | Video |
| 5. | D | T4 | Kraemer, pp. 21–23 |
| 6. | A | T4 | Kraemer, pp. 92–99 |
| 7. | D | V6 | Video |
| 8. | B | V6 | Video |
| 9. | B | V7 | Video |
| 10. | A | V7 | Video |
| 11. | B | V7 | Video |
| 12. | F | T4 | Kraemer, pp. 97–98 |
| 13. | | T1, T2, T3 | Kraemer, pp. 13–17 |
| 14. | | V6 | Video |
| 15. | | T4 | Kraemer, p. 99 |
| 16. | | T5 | Kraemer, pp. 100–104 |
| 17. | | T3, V6, V7 | Kraemer, pp. 21–25 |

# Lesson 7

# Community Involvement

## LESSON ASSIGNMENTS

Review the following assignments in order to schedule your time appropriately.

Text:

    There is no textbook reading assignment for this lesson.

Video:

    "Community Involvement" from the series *Texas Politics and You.*

Activities:

    One or more activities may be assigned to this lesson. Refer to your syllabus.

## OVERVIEW

Various theories of citizen participation and concepts of community are offered. Narration and expert commentary explain that citizen participation was once considered to be the cornerstone of democracy. Contemporary efforts to revive citizen participation and community action stem from several different motives: improving the quality of citizenship, reinvigorating political discourse, and moving the responsibility of solving society's problems from government to the private sector. Many people seem to believe community involvement and volunteerism are increasing. What are the benefits of people participating in community issues?

## LESSON GOAL

You should be able to analyze the meaning of citizenship and community involvement and determine how Texans can take an active part in shaping their lives.

# VIDEO OBJECTIVES

The following objectives are designed to help you get the most from the video segment of this lesson. Review them before watching the video. You may want to write notes to reinforce what you have learned.

1. Explain the value and importance of participation in a democracy and the function of the National Issues Convention.

2. Explain the goal and purpose of the Texas Family Pathfinder program and Mission Arlington.

3. Identify and evaluate the role of San Antonio's Communities Organized for Public Service (COPS), and assess what enabled them to achieve such a level of participatory politics.

4. Explain the dilemma that residents in Terlingua, Texas, faced and how they resolved it.

# PRACTICE TEST

After reading the assignment, watching the video, and addressing the objectives, you should be able to complete the following Practice Test. Some essay questions in this Practice Test may be included in your exams. When you have completed the Practice Test, turn to the Answer Key to score your answers.

MULTIPLE CHOICE

Select the single best answer. If more than one answer is required, it will be so indicated.

1. According to those who have studied the history of the United States, the tendency of Americans is to _____
   A. get involved in resolving community problems.
   B. ignore community problems and get engaged in national affairs.
   C. engage in international issues.
   D. avoid associations and volunteer organizations.

2. Mission Arlington _____
   A. serves the spiritual needs of its clients.
   B. assists with social needs such as clothing and food supplements.
   C. assists with building self-esteem.
   D. all of the above.

3. Communities Organized for Public Service (COPS) was successful in organizing the community _____
   A. to speak out against junkyards in their neighborhood.
   B. to lobby their city council to deal with the drainage and flooding problems in their neighborhood.
   C. to work with business leaders, educators, and city officials to found an educational partnership aimed at dropout prevention.
   D. all of the above.

4. The community in Terlingua, Texas, _____
   A. became a ghost town because of the vast exodus of residents.
   B. pulled together to get support from various levels of government and private funding.
   C. protested and marched at the capitol in Austin.
   D. fired their city council.

ESSAY PROBLEM QUESTIONS

5. Identify and evaluate the trends in the formation of neighborhood groups of people, churches, businesses, and government working together to solve community problems.

6. Using examples from the video, describe important assets and resources that are needed to make community activities successful.

# ANSWER KEY

The following provides the answers and references for the Practice Test questions. Objectives are referenced using the following abbreviations:

T=Textbook Objectives   V=Video Objectives

| Answer | Learning Objectives | References |
|---|---|---|
| 1. A | V1 | Video |
| 2. D | V2 | Video |
| 3. D | V3 | Video |
| 4. B | V4 | Video |
| 5. | V1, V2, V3, V4 | Video |
| 6. | V1, V2, V3, V4 | Video |

# Lesson 8

# Media and Public Agenda

## LESSON ASSIGNMENTS

Review the following assignments in order to schedule your time appropriately. For each lesson you will have a reading assignment and a video assignment.

Text:
    Kraemer, et al., *Texas Politics*, Chapter 4, "Political Parties," p. 94.

Video:
    "Media and Public Agenda" from the series *Texas Politics and You*.

Activities:
    One or more activities may be assigned to this lesson. Refer to your syllabus.

## OVERVIEW

The role of the media is examined to determine where and how citizens receive information about public issues. A democratic government would be virtually impossible without a free and active media to investigate improprieties, to publicize, and to explain ethical conduct of governmental officials and programs. The media has a public responsibility, but it also has power. Political officeholders and political interests are aware of the importance of the media. Press reports about specific topics and problems increase the level of awareness and put these issues in the spotlight where policy makers decide how to address them. Formulating informed choices regarding candidates and incumbent records have increasingly been based on media coverage. Politically diverse information is available through expanding media markets. Citizens must be able to determine the reliability and objectivity of news sources in a society where their participation in political decision making is expected.

# LESSON GOAL

You should be able to analyze how mass media influences the knowledge and attitudes of Texans toward public issues.

# TEXTBOOK OBJECTIVES

The following objectives are designed to help you get the most from the text. Review them before reading the assignment. You may want to write notes to reinforce what you have learned.

1. Explain the point of view expressed by the mass media in Texas.

2. Describe characteristics associated with Rush Limbaugh's talk radio.

# VIDEO OBJECTIVES

The following objectives are designed to help you get the most from the video segment of this lesson. Review them before watching the video. You may want to write notes to reinforce what you have learned.

3. Explain the importance of an independent press to a democratic society.

4. Identify and assess Molly Ivins' standards for political coverage.

5. Analyze the degree of influence the media has on public opinion, and assess the type of news content that is produced by newspapers.

6. Analyze the degree of influence the media has on public opinion, and assess the type of news content that is produced by television.

7. Use the example of Sylvester Turner's experience to analyze the degree of influence the media has in shaping public opinion and policy.

8. Assess the type of news content that is produced by talk radio.

9. Assess the type of news content that is produced via the Internet.

PRACTICE TEST

After reading the assignment, watching the video, and addressing the objectives, you should be able to complete the following Practice Test. Some essay questions in this Practice Test may be included in your exams. When you have completed the Practice Test, turn to the Answer Key to score your answers.

MULTIPLE CHOICE

Select the single best answer. If more than one answer is required, it will be so indicated.

1. According to the authors of *Texas Politics*, the tendency among the mass media in Texas is to _____
   A. echo the business point of view on most issues.
   B. rock the boat.
   C. favor liberal opinions.
   D. engage in personal attacks.
   E. reflect the growing minority interests.

2. By the 1990s Rush Limbaugh's talk-radio show was the main source of political news for _____
   A. less than 5 percent of the population.
   B. 26 percent of the population.
   C. 90 percent of the population.
   D. 50 percent of the female population.
   E. 50 percent of the male population.

3. The role of the media in a democratic society is to _____
   A. support the actions of governmental officials.
   B. present the facts about issues and officeholders.
   C. entertain the public.
   D. reflect the interests of corporate and conservative interests.

4. According to Molly Ivins, the political standards necessary for the mass media are _____
   A. no bias.
   B. accuracy and fairness.
   C. total objectivity.
   D. all of the above.

5. In the late 1990s, *The Dallas Morning News* followed a basic agenda that _____
   A. was strongly conservative.
   B. was socially progressive.
   C. avoided domestic issues regarding healthcare and social programs.
   D. concentrated on national and foreign news only.

6. Television has been criticized in its reporting of the news because it sometimes _____
   A. takes complex issues and reduces them to sound bites.
   B. concentrates on the image and not the substance.
   C. looks like a political attack ad.
   D. all of the above.

7. An example of television programming for the community would be the efforts made by _____
   A. KUBN to provide a voter registration campaign.
   B. North Texas Public Broadcasting to promote their agenda of educating and informing.
   C. Channel 8's goal of presenting diverse points of view.
   D. all of the above.

8. Sylvester Turner's campaign for mayor of Houston was _____
   A. aided by the heavy media coverage.
   B. ignored by the media.
   C. negatively impacted by a news story.
   D. only covered by talk radio.

9. The opportunity for citizens to engage in freedom of expression and an open flow of ideas is advanced by _____
   A. global information networks.
   B. governmental controls.
   C. commercial competition.
   D. all of the above.


ESSAY PROBLEM QUESTIONS

10. What is the relationship between political information and democracy? Is control of information a mechanism for maintaining political power?

11. Where can Americans get their most thorough and detailed analyses of political issues? Evaluate the different media sources for obtaining political information: TV, talk radio, print media, and the Internet.

12. Analyze the degree of influence the media has on public opinion. Compare the philosophy stated by reporters for *The Dallas Morning News* with the news coverage of the Sylvester Turner campaign. How was Sylvester Turner affected? How did he respond?

# ANSWER KEY

The following provides the answers and references for the Practice Test questions. Objectives are referenced using the following abbreviations:

T=Textbook Objectives   V=Video Objectives

| | Answer | Learning Objectives | References |
|---|---|---|---|
| 1. | A | T1 | Kraemer, p. 102 |
| 2. | B | T2 | Kraemer, p. 102 |
| 3. | B | V3 | Video |
| 4. | B | V4 | Video |
| 5. | B | V5 | Video |
| 6. | D | V6 | Video |
| 7. | D | V6 | Video |
| 8. | C | V7 | Video |
| 9. | A | V9 | Video |
| 10. | | V3 | Video |
| 11. | | V5, V6, V7, V8, V9 | Video |
| 12. | | V5, V6 | Video |

# Lesson 9

# Interest Groups in Texas

## LESSON ASSIGNMENTS

Review the following assignments in order to schedule your time appropriately. For each lesson you will have a reading assignment and a video assignment.

Text:
   Kraemer, et al., *Texas Politics*, Chapter 3, "Interest Groups," pp. 62–94.

Video:
   "Interest Groups in Texas" from the series *Texas Politics and You*.

Activities:
   One or more activities may be assigned to this lesson. Refer to your syllabus.

## OVERVIEW

In the Texas political system, interest groups targeting state decision makers in Austin have been a principal source of input making claims upon the institutions of government. Interest groups and their activities are seen as a necessary component of a democratic society; they also pose some problems and concerns. Not everyone has had equal access to the decision makers. Historically, and reflective of the traditionalistic-individualistic culture described earlier, the political demands receiving the most attention from policy makers have been from dominant economic interests who have participated actively in political campaigns and lobbying. The potential to become politically active remains open as we see people join together to focus and approach all levels of government. Uneven distribution of resources creates a challenge for Texas to respond to a broader citizen base.

# LESSON GOAL

You should be able to describe how interest groups can supplement the efforts of voters and parties in shaping decisions that affect individual lives, assess what accounts for interest groups' success or failure, and explain how the political system in Texas responds to the many and often conflicting demands.

# TEXTBOOK OBJECTIVES

The following objectives are designed to help you get the most from the text. Review them before reading the assignment. You may want to write notes to reinforce what you have learned.

1.  Define, classify, and assess the role of interest groups in a democratic society.

2.  Describe the various techniques used by interest groups to influence governmental policy, and assess the positive and or negative aspects of those activities.

3.  Explain two lessons learned in "Persuading the Public."

4.  Assess the impact interest groups have on administrative agencies.

5.  Explain how interest groups attempt to influence the judicial branch.

6.  Identify the major interest groups in Texas, and assess reasons for their successes.

7.  Explain the dilemma of lobby regulation.

# VIDEO OBJECTIVES

The following objectives are designed to help you get the most from the video segment of this lesson. Review them before watching the video. You may want to write notes to reinforce what you have learned.

8. Distinguish between a "contract" lobbyist and an "association" lobbyist, and explain what they consider as their most valuable resources for gaining support for their causes.

9. Explain two aspects of the Texas political system that critics claim make interest groups powerful in the state legislative process.

10. Explain how the efforts by Texans for Lawsuit Reform in 1995 and 1997 demonstrate both the power and limits of money.

11. Explain the goals and impact of the League of United Latin American Citizens (LULAC).

12. Give examples and explain how public-interest groups with little money can compete with groups with greater monetary resources.

13. Explain how people can accomplish political goals by listing the steps that were taken by a group of students called the Pearl Guards.

# PRACTICE TEST

After reading the assignment, watching the video, and addressing the objectives, you should be able to complete the following Practice Test. Some essay questions in this Practice Test may be included in your exams. When you have completed the Practice Test, turn to the Answer Key to score your answers.

## MULTIPLE CHOICE

Select the single best answer. If more than one answer is required, it will be so indicated.

1. Which of the following statements is NOT accurate with regard to the general rules of interest group formation?
   A. Those in the working class are more likely to join groups than those in the upper class.
   B. Economic-producing groups are more likely to be organized than are consuming groups.
   C. People with more education are more likely to join groups than those with less education.
   D. Passionate believers are more influential than citizens who are less emotionally involved.
   E. All of the statements above are accurate.

2. What is formed by an organization, industry, or individual for the purpose of collecting money and contributing to selected political candidates or causes?
   A. Political parties
   B. Political action committees
   C. Election committees
   D. Campaign committees
   E. None of the above

3. In attempting to influence the legislature, one of the most important resources lobbyists have available is _____
   A. information.
   B. connections.
   C. time.
   D. legal expertise.

4. Which industry's co-optation of a major regulatory board resulted in the legislature's decision in 1993 to abolish the board and give its regulatory powers to a single commissioner?
   A. The oil and gas industry
   B. The insurance industry
   C. The trucking industry
   D. The petrochemical industry
   E. The aerospace industry

5. The best known and probably the largest of the organizations that currently comprise the "Christian Right" is _____
   A. the Christian Coalition.
   B. the Moral Majority.
   C. Focus on the Family.
   D. the Family Research Council.
   E. the American Family Organization.

6. Labor unions are handicapped in Texas by state laws prohibiting _____
   A. closed shops.
   B. secondary boycotts.
   C. checkoff systems for union dues.
   D. mass picketing.
   E. all of the above.

7. The largest organization representing teachers in Texas is _____
   A. the Texas State Teachers Association.
   B. the Association of Professional Educators.
   C. the Texas Classroom Teachers Association.
   D. the Texas Federation of Teachers.
   E. none of the above.

8. Prior to the enactment of the 1991 "ethics bill," the most significant weakness of Texas laws designed to regulate legislative lobbying was that _____
   A. they were almost certainly unconstitutional.
   B. they covered only the most costly forms of lobbying.
   C. there was no agency charged with enforcing them.
   D. they pertained only to public-interest groups.
   E. they regulated only spending for entertainment.

9. In order to win support for their causes, lobbyists must _____
   A. remain indifferent and aloof to legislators.
   B. simply offer money for support.
   C. supply powerful arguments and good information.
   D. belong to an association.

10. The power of pooling money together to endorse a certain cause and candidate is enabled by _____
    A. political action committees.
    B. the revolving door policy.
    C. tort suits.
    D. all of the above.

11. A lesson to be learned from the experience of the Texans for Lawsuit Reform group is _____
    A. always make big investments in political campaigns.
    B. remind legislators that if an interest group demands change and they do not get it, that the money will not be there.
    C. money is not always the biggest factor in legislative politics.
    D. legislators like to be told how to vote.

12. One program that members of LULAC (League of United Latin American Citizens) were successful in getting the state legislatures to fund and then getting it adopted into the federal system is now known as _____
    A. Head Start.
    B. MADD.
    C. School Zones without Alcohol.
    D. Texans for Lawsuit Reform.

13. In order to advance their cause, the Pearl Guards _____
    A. protested at city hall.
    B. sought the help of a state legislator.
    C. researched laws to determine how to deal with their cause.
    D. all of the above.

## TRUE/FALSE

If the statement is true, write "T" to the left of the statement. If the statement (or any part of the statement) is false, write "F" to the left of the statement.

14. When people organize in an effort to influence the government to act in the private interest, democracy is strengthened since political participation of any type promotes democratic ideals.

15. A major function of administrative agencies is to protect the public interest by regulating various narrow, private interests.

16. The National Association for the Advancement of Colored People (NAACP) is an example of an interest group that promoted its interests effectively in the courts after having been unsuccessful in the legislative and executive branches.

17. Although public school teachers in Texas are divided among many different teachers' organizations, these organizations share the same goals and cooperate well with each other.

## ESSAY PROBLEM QUESTIONS

18. How do lobbyists go about trying to influence the legislative process? What restrictions does Texas law place on the activities of lobbyists? How do these restrictions affect the way interest groups operate in the state? How can the impact of interest groups be moderated?

19. What is co-optation? How does it occur? What are some of the problems that one might face in attempting to write legislation to minimize co-optation?

20. Which interest groups have the greatest influence on the policy making process in Texas? Which have the least influence? How would you explain this situation in terms of the state's political culture?

21. Discuss the basic role of interest groups in a democracy, and give examples of the sources of influence that make them effective. What lesson was learned from the experience that the Texans for Lawsuit Reform had?

22. What impact do public-interest groups have on legislation? What sources of influence can they bring to bear, and what are their limitations?

23. Profile the Pearl Guards and analyze their tactics and influence.

## ANSWER KEY

The following provides the answers and references for the Practice Test questions. Objectives are referenced using the following abbreviations:

T=Textbook Objectives   V=Video Objectives

| | Answer | Learning Objectives | References |
|---|---|---|---|
| 1. | A | T1 | Kraemer, pp. 64–65 |
| 2. | B | T2 | Kraemer, pp. 64–65 |
| 3. | A | T2 | Kraemer, pp. 67–73 |
| 4. | B | T4 | Kraemer, pp. 78–79 |
| 5. | A | T6 | Kraemer, p. 85 |
| 6. | E | T6 | Kraemer, pp. 87–88 |
| 7. | A | T6 | Kraemer, pp. 90–91 |
| 8. | C | T7 | Kraemer, p. 74 |
| 9. | C | V8 | Video |
| 10. | A | V9 | Video |
| 11. | C | V10 | Video |
| 12. | A | V11 | Video |
| 13. | D | V13 | Video |
| 14. | F | T1 | Kraemer, pp. 63–65 |
| 15. | T | T4 | Kraemer, p. 74 |
| 16. | T | T5 | Kraemer, p. 75 |
| 17. | F | T6 | Kraemer, p. 81 |
| 18. | | T1, T7 | Kraemer, pp. 67–75, 91–93 |
| 19. | | T4 | Kraemer, pp. 77–80 |
| 20. | | T6 | Kraemer, pp. 82–91 |
| 21. | | V8, V12 | Video |
| 22. | | V11, V12 | Video |
| 23. | | V13 | Video |

# Lesson 10

# Political Parties in Texas

## LESSON ASSIGNMENTS

Review the following assignments in order to schedule your time appropriately. For each lesson you will have a reading assignment and a video assignment.

Text:

> Kraemer, et al., *Texas Politics*, Chapter 4, "Political Parties," pp. 96–126.

Video:

> "Political Parties in Texas" from the series *Texas Politics and You*.

Activities:

> One or more activities may be assigned to this lesson. Refer to your syllabus.

## OVERVIEW

The study of political parties provides information about representative democracy. The parties in Texas perform a variety of functions: providing for and mobilizing citizenship participation in choosing public officials, developing a platform statement of principles and issues to address competing interests, and holding government accountable for its actions. To carry out these functions of organizing the electorate and winning control of the government, the parties have temporary and permanent party organizations. Numerous opportunities exist for parties to develop issues that educate and activate the public. When the party's candidate wins, the party is in the position to try and shape the direction of government by making policies that reflect the interest of their supporters. For most of the period since the Civil War, Texas functioned as a Democratic one-party state dominated by the conservative faction. Today, Texas has a two-party system. Both parties are challenged to seek a base of support that accommodates a range of ideological differences.

# LESSON GOAL

You should be able to define the functions and benefits of political parties, contrast the significant differences between the Texas Democratic and Texas Republican parties, and evaluate how well the party system in Texas performs these functions in organizing and linking citizens and government.

# TEXTBOOK OBJECTIVES

The following objectives are designed to help you get the most from the text. Review them before reading the assignment. You may want to write notes to reinforce what you have learned.

1. Explain the major interests that are associated with each party.

2. Explain why most Texans identified with the Democrats in the state's early history.

3. Explain the differences that generally occur in one-party systems and two-party systems.

4. Describe the functions that parties perform in their efforts to win elections.

5. Explain and assess how the temporary party organization facilitates participation in primaries and other party conventions.

6. Describe the functions of each element in the permanent party organization.

7. Explain why political parties in Texas are not "responsible parties."

8. Describe the characteristics of Republicans and conservative Democrats.

9. Explain what accounted for the Democratic Party's consistent success from the mid-1870s until the mid-1970s.

10. Describe the characteristics of liberal Democrats.

11. Explain why ideology has been more important than party affiliation in Texas.

---

# VIDEO OBJECTIVES

The following objectives are designed to help you get the most from the video segment of this lesson. Review them before watching the video. You may want to write notes to reinforce what you have learned.

12. Explain why the students joined the Young Democrats/Republicans and what they see as the role and function of political parties.

13. Analyze the role of political parties in providing and offering candidates for political office.

14. Explain how the special election in Congressional District 30 in Dallas was different and how it gives us a glimpse of what politics might be like if we did not have political parties.

15. Explain and give examples of the roles of Democratic and Republican local clubs.

16. Define *party platform* and how it is developed; compare and contrast the platforms of the Texas Democratic and Republican parties.

17. Identify the issues in the Oakley and Brown campaigns, and assess whether the winning candidate kept campaign promises.

## PRACTICE TEST

After reading the assignment, watching the video, and addressing the objectives, you should be able to complete the following Practice Test. Some essay questions in this Practice Test may be included in your exams. When you have completed the Practice Test, turn to the Answer Key to score your answers.

MULTIPLE CHOICE

Select the single best answer. If more than one answer is required, it will be so indicated.

1.  Those interests who tend to be the target of lawsuits are _____
    A.  doctors and business owners who have leaned toward Democratic candidates.
    B.  doctors and business owners who are opposed to tort reform.
    C.  doctors and business owners who have leaned toward Republican candidates.
    D.  injured people who tend to favor Republican candidates opposing tort reform.

2.  Which party did most Texans come to identify with after Reconstruction ended?
    A.  Federalist
    B.  Whig
    C.  Republican
    D.  Democratic
    E.  Populist

3.  The first Republican governor of Texas in the twentieth century was _____
    A.  John Tower.
    B.  John Connally.
    C.  Bill Clements.
    D.  Phil Gramm.
    E.  Clayton Williams.

4. The basic function of political parties is to _____
   A. recruit political leaders.
   B. stimulate political activity and provide information.
   C. moderate differences between groups.
   D. organize the decision making activities of government.
   E. win elections in order to gain control over public policy.

5. In Texas, party membership is determined by _____
   A. the payment of dues.
   B. the act of voting.
   C. the indication of party preference on the voter registration card.
   D. attendance at a party convention.
   E. none of the above.

6. The state Democratic convention selects all of the following EXCEPT _____
   A. the party nominees for the general election in November.
   B. the presidential electors to serve in the electoral college.
   C. the members of the State Democratic Executive Committee.
   D. the Texas members of the Democratic National Committee.
   E. the delegates to the Democratic National Convention.

7. Which of the following is responsible for conducting the party primary elections in Texas?
   A. The precinct chair
   B. The county executive committee
   C. The district executive committee
   D. The state executive committee
   E. None of the above

8. Republicans in Texas tend overwhelmingly to be concentrated in _____
   A. urban and suburban areas.
   B. small towns.
   C. farm areas.
   D. Hispanic communities.
   E. none of the above.

9. Conservative Democrats won almost every public election in Texas from the 1870s to the 1970s because _____
   A. their supporters have had both the time and money to devote to politics.
   B. smaller percentages of liberals than conservatives vote in Texas.
   C. they have frequently written party rules to their own advantage.
   D. the open primary system favored conservative candidates.
   E. all of the above factors.

10. Which of the following political factions has been helped most by labor unions?
   A. Liberal Republicans
   B. Conservative Republicans
   C. Liberal Democrats
   D. Conservative Democrats
   E. None of the above

11. The students saw the role and function of political parties as a way to _____
   A. educate people about issues and candidates.
   B. provide an avenue for people to be involved in their government.
   C. to motivate and excite people.
   D. all of the above.

12. What is the role of the party in offering candidates for political office?
   A. Parties engage in recruiting candidates but never assist with financial resources.
   B. Parties help educate them in how to run effective campaigns.
   C. Parties screen and deny the party label to those who do not support the party platform.
   D. All of the above

13. The voters in Congressional District 30 in Dallas County were faced with a different election because _____
   A. there was no one running for that seat.
   B. there were only Democrats on the ballot.
   C. there were only Republicans on the ballot.
   D. there were eight names of Democrats, Republicans, and Independents on the ballot.

14. The White Rock/Lake Highlands Democrats is a grassroots organization that _____
    A. is dedicated to youth issues.
    B. works to bring people together by discussing candidates and community issues.
    C. recruits only women candidates.
    D. officially collects information and utilizes the Internet to target representatives in Washington.

15. The Democratic Party in Texas stresses _____
    A. a commitment to clean air and clean water.
    B. keeping government out of peoples' lives.
    C. a pro-life position.
    D. reduced governmental spending.

16. Once elected to office, Representative Keith Oakley _____
    A. did not try to pass legislation that reflected his campaign promises.
    B. filed legislation such as funding for Tawakoni State Park that would provide benefits for his district.
    C. filed legislation that would increase property taxes.
    D. became more concerned with how his vote on major issues would be interpreted in the next election.

TRUE/FALSE

If the statement is true, write "T" to the left of the statement. If the statement (or any part of the statement) is false, write "F" to the left of the statement.

17. Although Republicans have made considerable gains in recent years, Texas voters who identify themselves as Democrats still greatly outnumber those who identify themselves as Republicans.

18. One of the functions of the state convention is to write the party platform.

19. Because American political parties have centralized control over nominations and financing and can require that their members support the party platform, they may be considered "responsible parties."

20. From a socioeconomic standpoint, the liberal faction of the Democratic Party tends to be more homogeneous than the conservative faction.

## ESSAY PROBLEM QUESTIONS

21. Analyze the platforms of the Texas Democratic and Texas Republican parties, and identify significant ideological and policy differences.

22. What are the major functions of political parties? How well do political parties in Texas perform these functions? What factors, if any, suggest that the parties are improving in their performance of these functions?

23. Describe briefly the development of the political party system in Texas from the period of the Republic of Texas to the present. What accounts for the dominance of the conservative Democrats during most of this history? Why has the dominance been eroding in recent years?

24. Describe the structures and primary functions of the permanent party organization of the Democratic Party in Texas. What are some of the factors that make the permanent party organization less important than might be expected?

25. Explain the changes that the residents of Congressional District 30 faced when they went to the polls in November. How did this election impact the voters and the political party process?

26. Do candidates keep their campaign promises? Use the Brown and Oakley campaigns to explain your assessment.

# ANSWER KEY

The following provides the answers and references for the Practice Test questions.
Objectives are referenced using the following abbreviations:
T=Textbook Objectives   V=Video Objectives

|  | Answer | Learning Objectives | References |
|---|---|---|---|
| 1. | C | T1 | Kraemer, p. 103 |
| 2. | D | T2 | Kraemer, p. 103 |
| 3. | C | T3 | Kraemer, p. 104 |
| 4. | E | T4 | Kraemer, p. 108 |
| 5. | B | T5 | Kraemer, p. 111 |
| 6. | A | T5 | Kraemer, pp. 111–112 |
| 7. | B | T6 | Kraemer, pp. 111–113 |
| 8. | A | T8 | Kraemer, pp. 106–108 |
| 9. | E | T9 | Kraemer, p. 106 |
| 10. | A | T10 | Kraemer, pp. 118–119 |
| 11. | D | V12 | Video |
| 12. | B | V13 | Video |
| 13. | D | V14 | Video |
| 14. | B | V15 | Video |
| 15. | A | V16 | Video |
| 16. | B | V17 | Video |
| 17. | F | T3 | Kraemer, pp. 106–108 |
| 18. | T | T5 | Kraemer, p. 112 |
| 19. | F | T7 | Kraemer, p. 115 |
| 20. | F | T10 | Kraemer, pp. 119–121 |
| 21. | | T1, T3, T11 | Kraemer, pp. 109–110 |
| 22. | | T4, T5, T6, V16 | Kraemer, pp. 108–110; Video |
| 23. | | T2, T3, T9 | Kraemer, pp. 104–108 |
| 24. | | T5, T6, T7 | Kraemer, pp. 114–115 |
| 25. | | V14 | Video |
| 26. | | V17 | Video |

# Lesson 11

# Third Parties in Texas

## LESSON ASSIGNMENTS

Review the following assignments in order to schedule your time appropriately. For each lesson you will have a reading assignment and a video assignment.

Text:

Kraemer, et al., *Texas Politics*, Chapter 4, "Political Parties," pp. 122–124.

Video:

"Third Parties in Texas" from the series *Texas Politics and You*.

Activities:

One or more activities may be assigned to this lesson. Refer to your syllabus.

## OVERVIEW

In view of the size and diversity of interests in Texas, it is interesting to look at why political competition has been dominated by just two major political parties. Third parties have competed for power but many minor or third parties are unknown to most people. They are small and are not around for any long periods of times. As of 1997, no Texas third party has ever had statewide electoral success. Factions, economic reforms, and doctrines to advance new ideas toward solving social and economic challenges have generated the bases for the formation of minor parties. However, state and federal laws written by Democratic and Republican legislators have made it difficult for minor parties to effectively compete with the two parties. Nevertheless, third parties continue to appear on the scene; third-party contenders in Texas have been La Raza Unida and the Libertarian Party. Also, the Reform Party that grew out of the movement to elect Ross Perot has been successful in organizing and gaining access to the ballot. On broad policy issues, the electorate tends to cluster near the center, and that is where the two major parties have already established themselves, thus leaving little room for third parties to make a lasting niche.

## LESSON GOAL

You should be able to describe reasons for third-party successes and failures and assess the impact on the political arena in Texas.

## TEXTBOOK OBJECTIVES

The following objectives are designed to help you get the most from the text. Review them before reading the assignment. You may want to write notes to reinforce what you have learned.

1.  Assess why third parties appear on the political scene.

2.  Explain and evaluate the process that new parties must follow to be listed on the ballot.

3.  Describe the political philosophy of the Libertarian Party and assess its future.

4.  Explain the significance of La Raza Unida.

## VIDEO OBJECTIVES

The following objectives are designed to help you get the most from the video segment of this lesson. Review them before watching the video. You may want to write notes to reinforce what you have learned.

5.  Briefly explain the goals of the American Constitution Party, the Texas Labor Party, the Reform Party, the Libertarian Party, the Natural Law Party, and La Raza Unida.

6.  List three reasons for the appearance of third parties. Give examples for each.

7.  Discuss the history and impact of La Raza Unida.

8. Explain five reasons why statewide electoral success for third parties has been extremely difficult in Texas.

9. Assess the contributions of third parties.

## PRACTICE TEST

After reading the assignment, watching the video, and addressing the objectives, you should be able to complete the following Practice Test. Some essay questions in this Practice Test may be included in your exams. When you have completed the Practice Test, turn to the Answer Key to score your answers.

MULTIPLE CHOICE

Select the single best answer. If more than one answer is required, it will be so indicated.

1. How do third parties generally influence the political system?
   A. They usually win easy access to the ballot and thus offer the voters a variety of viewpoints.
   B. They generally draw support from Anglo middle and upper classes and thus win significant races.
   C. They usually achieve permanent status.
   D. Their positions and platforms are sometimes adopted by the two major parties.

2. A person nominated for statewide office by one of the major parties in Texas _____
   A. must collect signatures totaling 1 percent of the total votes cast in the last gubernatorial election.
   B. must collect signatures from registered voters who did not participate in a primary or runoff that year.
   C. is automatically accorded a spot on the ballot.
   D. both A and B.

3. The Libertarian Party in Texas _____
   A. ✓ opposes almost all government involvement in both economic and personal life.
   B. believes that both parties do not provide enough services for the well-being of the people.
   C. favors more governmental regulations in the economy.
   D. favors more governmental restrictions on abortion to protect the unborn.

4. The political party that successfully won some local elections and represented Mexican Americans in Texas was _____
   A. LULAC — League of United Latin American Citizens.
   B. the American GI Forum.
   C. MAD — the Mexican American Democrats.
   D. ✓ La Raza Unida — "The United Race."

5. The characterization of being "fiscally conservative and socially moderate" is one that is favored by the _____
   A. American Constitution Party.
   B. Texas Labor Party.
   C. ✓ Reform Party.
   D. Libertarian Party.

6. The Libertarian Party is often given as an example of one that formed around _____
   A. powerful personalities.
   B. ✓ ideology.
   C. protest.
   D. none of the above.

7. The 1972 campaign and election is significant to La Raza Unida because _____
   A. their candidate won the gubernatorial seat.
   B. their candidate caused the Democrat candidate for governor to lose to the Republican candidate.
   C. ✓ their candidate won enough votes to deny the Democratic nominee for governor a majority for the first time in the twentieth century.
   D. their party won a school board election for the first time.

8. ✓The winner-take-all system _____
   A. makes it difficult for third parties to ever get represented.
   B. makes it easier for third parties to compete.
   C. means that many candidates can win seats in a district election.
   D. means that the party that gets the most votes in a district can appoint all the legislators for that district.

9. ✓Third parties _____
   A. offer voters more choices.
   B. provide new ideas for the two major parties to consider.
   C. provide outlets for protest and frustration.
   D. all of the above.


ESSAY PROBLEM QUESTIONS

10. Assess why third parties appear, and give three reasons to explain their limited successes in Texas.

11. Explain the strategy Libertarians have used to maintain a place on the ballot, and assess their chances for continual success in the electoral arena.

12. Discuss the significance and impact of La Raza Unida.

# ANSWER KEY

The following provides the answers and references for the Practice Test questions. Objectives are referenced using the following abbreviations:

T=Textbook Objectives   V=Video Objectives

| | Answer | Learning Objectives | References |
|---|---|---|---|
| 1. | D | T1 | Kraemer, p. 122 |
| 2. | C | T2 | Kraemer, p. 123 |
| 3. | A | T3 | Kraemer, p. 123 |
| 4. | D | T4 | Kraemer, p. 124 |
| 5. | C | V5 | Video |
| 6. | B | V6 | Video |
| 7. | C | V7 | Video |
| 8. | A | V8 | Video |
| 9. | D | V9 | Video |
| 10. | | T1, T2, T4 | Kraemer, pp. 122–124 |
| 11. | | T3 | Kraemer, p. 123 |
| 12. | | T4, V7 | Video |

# Lesson 12

# Campaigns and Elections

## LESSON ASSIGNMENTS

Review the following assignments in order to schedule your time appropriately. For each lesson you will have a reading assignment and a video assignment.

Text:

Kraemer, et al., *Texas Politics*, Chapter 5, "Campaigns and Elections," pp. 128–156

Video:

"Campaigns and Elections" from the series *Texas Politics and You*.

Activities:

One or more activities may be assigned to this lesson. Refer to your syllabus.

## OVERVIEW

Free and open campaigns are considered to be important elements of democracy in action. Throughout the United States approximately a half-million persons hold elected state and local offices. In Texas, we hold elections for everything from state judges to county sheriffs. Elections embody such values as free speech, majority rule, and political equality and serve important functions such as allowing people to remove and choose leaders in a peaceful manner, to shape the direction of government, and promote political appreciation and attachment to the system of government. Voters can influence important issues through their choices as seen specifically in a closer look at school board campaigns. School board elections, which traditionally have low voter turnout, have experienced contested seats and ideological debates, and the campaign gives voters the chance to learn about the personal qualities of the candidates. The struggle to influence state and local education policy includes many strategies such as forming PACs to raise money and organizing phone banks and mailings. Campaigns to inform often turn negative. School board elections are important to study to understand the vital need for participation from all and to realize how the usual low voter turnout can allow for a disproportionate influence of a few individuals.

## LESSON GOAL

You should be able to explain why campaigns and elections are important in a democracy.

## TEXTBOOK OBJECTIVES

The following objectives are designed to help you get the most from the text. Review them before reading the assignment. You may want to write notes to reinforce what you have learned.

1. Assess the character of campaigns, and explain why campaigns focus on symbols and appealing images.

2. Explain why people and money are two essential campaign resources.

3. Evaluate how campaign money influences public policy.

4. Describe and assess efforts to control the impact of money in campaigns.

5. Define *negative campaigning*, and explain how it harms democracy.

6. Assess the impact that Texas political parties have on candidates.

7. Explain the purpose and procedure for conducting primaries in Texas.

8. Describe the purpose and procedure for holding general and special elections.

9. Describe the strategies of the 1994 election, and assess the impact of the outcomes.

## VIDEO OBJECTIVES

The following objectives are designed to help you get the most from the video segment of this lesson. Review them before watching the video. You may want to write notes to reinforce what you have learned.

10. List four functions that political consultant Karl Rove gives to explain the benefits of campaigns and elections in a democracy.

11. Explain why Morris Overstreet and Rick Perry each decided to become candidates and run for public offices. Compare and contrast their campaign strategies.

12. Explain the concern over low voter turnout. Discuss the nonpartisan school board election in Cypress-Fairbanks, and assess the campaign strategies of FOCUS and the school board candidates. What factors determined the outcome?

13. Explain and assess the purpose of the formation of the Texas Freedom Network and the Christian Coalition.

# PRACTICE TEST

After reading the assignment, watching the video, and addressing the objectives, you should be able to complete the following Practice Test. Some essay questions in this Practice Test may be included in your exams. When you have completed the Practice Test, turn to the Answer Key to score your answers.

MULTIPLE CHOICE

Select the single best answer. If more than one answer is required, it will be so indicated.

1.  Regardless of their strategies, the resources all political candidates must have are _____
    A.  time and money.
    B.  ✓people and money.
    C.  time and information.
    D.  media and information.
    E.  polling data and money.

2.  The Texas Campaign Reporting and Disclosure Act of 1973 requires that every candidate for political office appoint a(n) _____ before accepting contributions or making expenditures.
    A.  campaign manager
    B.  ✓campaign treasurer
    C.  legal adviser
    D.  interest group liaison
    E.  ethics counselor

3.  The ethics bill passed by the Texas legislature in 1991 _____
    A.  limits campaign contributions in all state elections.
    B.  limits campaign contributions only in judicial elections.
    C.  limits campaign contributions only in legislative elections.
    D.  limits campaign contributions only in gubernatorial elections.
    E.  ✓does not place any limits on campaign contributions.

4. Candidates use negative campaigning _____
   A. to emphasize public policy.
   B. to encourage voters to participate on election day.
   C. because they believe such tactics are effective.
   D. it encourages more good people to enter public life.

5. The Texas Election Code requires any political party whose candidate for governor received at least _____ in the most recent general election to hold a primary to choose candidates for upcoming elections.
   A. 500,000 votes
   B. 1,000,000 votes
   C. 10 percent of the vote
   D. 20 percent of the vote
   E. 30 percent of the vote

6. General elections in Texas are held on the Tuesday after the first Monday in _____ in even-numbered years.
   A. March
   B. May
   C. September
   D. November
   E. none of the above

7. Richard Fisher defeated _____ in a 1994 runoff to win the Democratic nomination for U.S. Senate.
   A. Kay Bailey Hutchison
   B. Mike Andrews
   C. Jim Mattox
   D. Raul Gonzalez
   E. Bob Krueger

8. Why do we have elections?
   A. To give citizens a chance to elect those candidates who offer programs they prefer
   B. To replace leaders that citizens object to in a peaceable manner
   C. To remind those in power that they can be held accountable
   D. All of the above

9. Rick Perry was motivated to participate in the electoral process because _____
   A. ✓his family has been involved in public service for many generations.
   B. he grew up at a time prior to integration and believed that the key to progress required involvement in decision making.
   C. he needed a job.
   D. he wanted to be a judge.

10. The aim of the group called FOCUS is to _____
    A. educate and activate.
    B. support a unified school calendar.
    C. oppose a year-round school calendar.
    D. ✓all of the above.

11. According to Jeff Fisher, the goal of the Christian Coalition is to _____
    A. train and equip people of faith on how the political process works.
    B. endorse candidates.
    C. identify conservative people who wish to be involved.
    D. ✓A and C only.


TRUE/FALSE

If the statement is true, write "T" to the left of the statement. If the statement (or any part of the statement) is false, write "F" to the left of the statement.

12. T Clayton Williams captured the Republican nomination for governor in 1990 in large part because of the powerful visual images he used to capitalize on the public's fear of crime.

13. F Politicians generally favor the system of private campaign financing that prevails in the United States.

14. F Party platforms generally provide an accurate guide to what candidates plan to do if elected.

15. T In spite of significant gains by the Republicans in the 1994 general elections, Democrats retained their majorities in the Texas Senate and House of Representatives.

## ESSAY PROBLEM QUESTIONS

16. What are the implications for democracy of private financing of election campaigns? What has been done in Texas to try to control money in campaigns? What, if anything, should be done by the state to improve campaign finance regulation?

17. Describe an example of negative campaigning, and explain four reasons it is harmful to democracy.

18. Explain and assess the role of elections in Texas.

19. Explain, with examples from the video, what is meant by the statement that "we can elect people to public office both by our silence and our support."

20. Discuss and assess the goals of the Texas Freedom Network, and analyze the political and practical reasons that candidates aligned with the religious right would focus election efforts on school board elections.

# ANSWER KEY

The following provides the answers and references for the Practice Test questions. Objectives are referenced using the following abbreviations:

T=Textbook Objectives   V=Video Objectives

| | Answer | Learning Objectives | References |
|---|---|---|---|
| 1. | B | T2 | Kraemer, pp. 136–137 |
| 2. | B | T4 | Kraemer, p. 141 |
| 3. | E | T4 | Kraemer, p. 142 |
| 4. | C | T5 | Kraemer, pp. 144–145 |
| 5. | D | T7 | Kraemer, p. 145 |
| 6. | D | T8 | Kraemer, p. 147 |
| 7. | C | T9 | Kraemer, p. 149 |
| 8. | D | V10 | Video |
| 9. | A | V11 | Video |
| 10. | D | V12 | Video |
| 11. | D | V13 | Video |
| 12. | T | T1 | Kraemer, pp. 144–145 |
| 13. | F | T3 | Kraemer, p. 138 |
| 14. | F | T6 | Kraemer, pp. 108–110 |
| 15. | T | T9 | Kraemer, p. 149 |
| 16. | | T3, T4 | Kraemer, pp. 137–144 |
| 17. | | T5 | Kraemer, pp. 144–145 |
| 18. | | V10, V11 | Video |
| 19. | | V12, V13 | Video |
| 20. | | V13 | Video |

# Lesson 13

# The Ballot Box: Voting under Texas Law

## LESSON ASSIGNMENTS

Review the following assignments in order to schedule your time appropriately. For each lesson you will have a reading assignment and a video assignment.

Text:

Kraemer, et al., *Texas Politics*, Chapter 5, "Campaigns and Elections," pp. 129–154.

Video:

"The Ballot Box: Voting under Texas Law" from the series *Texas Politics and You*.

Activities:

One or more activities may be assigned to this lesson. Refer to your syllabus.

## OVERVIEW

The role of voting is emphasized from the standpoint of the individual and the political system. You will look at the historical evolution of voting to understand how antidemocratic schemes to restrict voter participation were eventually defeated. Major characteristics of the current system of voter registration in Texas can be compared to systems of registration previously used by the state. Reasons for Texans not voting will be explored, and you should assess what effect significantly higher voter turnout would have on state politics.

## LESSON GOAL

You should be able to analyze the role of voting in a democratic political system and assess the reasons for low voter turnout in Texas.

## TEXTBOOK OBJECTIVES

The following objectives are designed to help you get the most from the text. Review them before reading the assignment. You may want to write notes to reinforce what you have learned.

1. Explain why voting is important from the standpoint of a democratic political system.

2. Describe how the right to vote has been expanded.

3. Assess how voter registration procedures encourage or discourage voting.

4. Explain why Texans do not vote, and assess the impact of low voter turnout.

## VIDEO OBJECTIVES

The following objectives are designed to help you get the most from the video segment of this lesson. Review them before watching the video. You may want to write notes to reinforce what you have learned.

5. Explain why voter turnout among minorities has been historically low in Texas, and assess reasons why low voter turnout continues in spite of the Voting Rights Act of 1965.

6. Discuss the concerns that Mexican American Legal Defense and Educational Fund (MALDEF) spokesperson Nina Perales has regarding the inquiry into citizenship, and assess whether electoral regulations in Texas are "progressive."

7. Discuss socioeconomic and other factors such as Project Vote that are likely to influence people to register and vote.

8. Assess the impact that voting has on the selection of leaders and the implementation of policies.

9. Explain why laws to curb election fraud were needed in Texas, and assess whether the reforms can reduce fraud without restricting voting rights.

10. Explain how districting for city council seats and gender issues relate to voting representation.


PRACTICE TEST


After reading the assignment, watching the video, and addressing the objectives, you should be able to complete the following Practice Test. Some essay questions in this Practice Test may be included in your exams. When you have completed the Practice Test, turn to the Answer Key to score your answers.

MULTIPLE CHOICE

Select the single best answer. If more than one answer is required, it will be so indicated.

1. The primary reason most people vote is that they _____
   A. believe that their vote may determine the outcome of the election.
   B. understand the importance of voting as a means of decreasing alienation.
   C. wish to confer legitimacy on democratically elected officeholders.
   D. view a large turnout as a means of preventing dishonesty in elections.
   E. have been taught to believe that voting is their duty.

2. Poll taxes, white-only primaries, and literacy tests were all designed to _____
   A. increase voter turnout rates.
   B. discourage voting by African Americans, Mexican Americans, and poor whites.
   C. eliminate voter fraud in local elections.
   D. encourage two-party competition.
   E. none of the above.

3. The Twenty-fourth Amendment to the U.S. Constitution outlawed _____
   A. white-only primaries.
   B. property qualifications for voting.
   C. annual registration requirements for voting.
   D. ✓the poll tax.
   E. all of the above.

4. Voter turnout in Texas is _____
   A. above the national average.
   B.✓ below the national average.
   C. approximately the same as the national average.
   D. above the national average for presidential elections but below for others.
   E. below the national average for presidential elections but above for others.

5. The level of political participation and voter turnout in Texas and in other states of the Old South is increasing in response to the _____
   A. declining partisanship of the state's media.
   B. increasing influence of the traditionalistic political culture.
   C. increasing emphasis on improving public education.
   D. ✓increasing level of activity of the Republican party.
   E. all of the above.

6. When minorities in Texas fail to vote, what candidates are hurt most?
   A. ✓Liberal Democratic
   B. Conservative Democratic
   C. Republican
   D. Independent
   E. None of the above

7. Immediately after the Civil War during Reconstruction, political participation by African Americans in Texas _____
   A. did not exist.
   B. increased—many were now voting and were members of the Republican Party.
   C. included running, winning, and holding public offices.
   D. ✓both B and C.

8. Texas has become more progressive in its electoral regulations because _____

   A. it has devised lengthy and costly mechanisms to ensure that only people with high incomes and property will vote.
   B. its laws require annual registration, fees, and literacy tests.
   C. ✓ it has complied with federal laws to provide voting registration materials in departments of public safety and other accessible places.
   D. its laws require proof of citizenship and have prosecuted many noncitizens who have voted.

9. According to Secretary of State Antonio Garza, voters turn out at a higher rate when there are _____
   A. issues like the lottery.
   B. issues that benefit a particular community.
   C. issues where competing interests might lose if change occurred.
   D. ✓ all of the above.

10. Increasing the convenience of voting in Texas even further _____
    A. is not desired by officials because of the fear of fraud.
    B. ✓ is a hopeful goal that includes incorporating changes in technology such as touch television screen.
    C. is a hopeful goal which includes a poll tax.
    D. is not seen as a way to increase voter turnout.

11. When Ann Richards ran for governor in 1990, _____
    A. she drew support from minorities.
    B. she drew support from women.
    C. she drew support from those who advocated equality.
    D. ✓ all of the above.

12. Electoral fraud in the 1990s _____
    A. did not occur because very few people voted.
    B. ✓ involved the intercepting of absentee mail ballots.
    C. involved many noncitizens who were registering to vote.
    D. involved computer theft and changing the numerical outcomes.

13. In 1991, the City of Dallas was ordered by a federal judge to _____
    A. have at-large elections for all seats on the city council.
    B. ✓ restructure the at-large district elections to provide a system that would allow for more minority representation.
    C. appoint women and minorities to positions of power.
    D. appoint white males to positions of power.

TRUE/FALSE

If the statement is true, write "T" to the left of the statement. If the statement (or any part of the statement) is false, write "F" to the left of the statement.

14. Under current Texas law, one must register between October 1 and January 31 to be eligible to vote.

ESSAY PROBLEM QUESTIONS

15. Briefly trace the extension of suffrage in the United States and Texas, and assess the impact of past discrimination on voter turnout in Texas today. Will projects such as Project Vote make a difference? What other actions can the state take to improve voter turnout?

16. What are the major characteristics of the current system of voter registration in Texas? Do you consider the state's present registration requirements to be a significant barrier to voting? How does the current system compare to systems of registration previously used by the state?

17. What specific recommendations would you make to increase the level of political participation in Texas? What effect would significantly higher voter turnout have on state politics?

18. Explain why Texans seem to participate and vote less frequently than residents of other states.

19. Identify and explain why some people vote and others do not. Explain why voter turnout in Texas is below the national average. What is Texas doing to increase voter turnout?

20. Discuss the election of Ann Richards, discuss the significance of restructuring district elections for city council seats, and explain how voting affects leadership and public policy.

## ANSWER KEY

The following provides the answers and references for the Practice Test questions. Objectives are referenced using the following abbreviations:

T=Textbook Objectives   V=Video Objectives

| | Answer | Learning Objectives | References |
|---|---|---|---|
| 1. | E | T1 | Kraemer, p. 129 |
| 2. | B | T2 | Kraemer, pp. 130–131 |
| 3. | D | T3 | Kraemer, p. 131 |
| 4. | B | T4 | Kraemer, p. 132 |
| 5. | D | T4 | Kraemer, p. 133 |
| 6. | A | T4 | Kraemer, p. 134 |
| 7. | D | V5 | Video |
| 8. | C | V6 | Video |
| 9. | D | V7 | Video |
| 10. | B | V7 | Video |
| 11. | D | V8 | Video |
| 12. | B | V9 | Video |
| 13. | B | V10 | Video |
| 14. | F | T3 | Kraemer, pp. 131–132 |
| 15. | | T2, V8 | Kraemer, p. 130; Video |
| 16. | | T3 | Kraemer, pp. 131–132 |
| 17. | | T3 | Kraemer, pp. 132–136 |
| 18. | | T4 | Kraemer, pp. 132–136 |
| 19. | | V6, V7 | Video |
| 20. | | V8, V10 | Video |

# Lesson 14

# The Texas Legislature

## LESSON ASSIGNMENTS

Review the following assignments in order to schedule your time appropriately. For each lesson you will have a reading assignment and a video assignment.

Text:

     Kraemer, et al., *Texas Politics*, Chapter 6, "Organization of the Texas Legislature," pp. 158–192 and Chapter 7, "The Legislative Process," pp. 194–222.

Video:

     "The Texas Legislature" from the series *Texas Politics and You*.

Activities:

     One or more activities may be assigned to this lesson. Refer to your syllabus.

## OVERVIEW

The Texas legislature faces the challenge of resolving a vast range of public problems in a relatively short period of time. The Texas Constitution stipulates that the legislature is to meet only once every two years and further limits it to 140 days at that time. A limited biennial session with volumes of bills, part-time legislators, and many outside influences raises questions of whether there is sufficient time for research and proper review. Rules have been adopted by both houses that grant the presiding officers extensive procedural authority. Committees and leadership roles play a significant part in meeting the workload demands and policy making in Texas. When the management of the state's needs are not completed, the governor can call the legislature into special session. Calls for term limits and initiative and referendum illustrate the concern over balancing power in the legislative process.

# LESSON GOAL

You should be able to describe the organization of the Texas legislature, identify those who exercise power, and explain how and why they have control over the process.

# TEXTBOOK OBJECTIVES

The following objectives are designed to help you get the most from the text. Review them before reading the assignment. You may want to write notes to reinforce what you have learned.

1. Describe the structure and size of the Texas legislature and the members' terms of office.

2. Explain what the Texas Constitution stipulates about regular and called sessions.

3. Explain the purpose of redistricting, and describe the role the legislature and the courts have played.

4. Assess the significance of political party affiliation on the legislative process in Texas.

5. Evaluate the level of compensation that legislators receive.

6. Describe the characteristics of the average Texas state legislator, and assess how representative the legislature is.

7. Describe the roles of the lieutenant governor, speaker of the House, and the pro tempore positions.

8. Explain the purpose of the five basic types of committees in the Texas legislature.

9. Assess the role of the Texas legislative staff.

10. Describe the criticism that is levied against the Texas legislature, and explain the impact that suggested reforms would have.

11. Describe the powers of the presiding officers.

12. Describe the factors that prevent the presiding officers from having absolute power.

## VIDEO OBJECTIVES

The following objectives are designed to help you get the most from the video segment of this lesson. Review them before watching the video. You may want to write notes to reinforce what you have learned.

13. Assess the impact that a limited biennial session has on the rules that provide powers to the presiding officers.

14. Describe the powers that are held by the lieutenant governor in the Texas Senate.

15. Describe the powers of the speaker of the House in Texas, and assess how that power was used by Speakers Laney and Lewis.

16. Contrast the different styles of Lieutenant Governor Hobby and Lieutenant Governor Bullock.

17. Assess the impact that term limits and initiative and referendum would have on the legislative process and the presiding officers.

# PRACTICE TEST

After reading the assignment, watching the video, and addressing the objectives, you should be able to complete the following Practice Test. Some essay questions in this Practice Test may be included in your exams. When you have completed the Practice Test, turn to the Answer Key to score your answers.

## MULTIPLE CHOICE

Select the single best answer. If more than one answer is required, it will be so indicated.

1. The number of members in the Texas House of Representatives is _____
   A. 50.
   B. 100.
   C. 131.
   D. √150.
   E. 435.

2. Special sessions of the Texas legislature called by the governor are limited to a maximum of how many days?
   A. 10
   B. √30
   C. 50
   D. 60
   E. 90

3. If the Texas legislature fails to redistrict, responsibility for redistricting is assumed by _____
   A. the governor.
   B. the Texas Legislative Council.
   C. √the Legislative Redistricting Board.
   D. the General Land Office.
   E. none of the above.

4. Which of the following statements concerning party organization in the Texas legislature is NOT correct?
   A. ✓ There are no party caucuses in the legislature.
   B. Both Democrats and Republicans chair standing committees in the legislature.
   C. The presiding officers of the legislature generally de-emphasize partisanship.
   D. Party floor leaders have existed in the House for less than two decades.
   E. Party divisions are much less important in the Texas legislature than in the U.S. Congress.

5. The current salary for legislators in Texas was established by _____
   A. the governor.
   B. the legislature.
   C. the Texas Supreme Court.
   D. ✓ a constitutional amendment.
   E. none of the above.

6. The average age of state legislators in Texas is approximately _____
   A. 35.
   B. 40.
   C. ✓ 50.
   D. 60.
   E. 65.

7. The speaker of the Texas House of Representatives is chosen by the _____
   A. electorate.
   B. governor.
   C. ✓ members of the House.
   D. lieutenant governor.
   E. none of the above.

8. Which committees in the Texas legislature most closely resemble select committees in the U.S. Congress?
   A. Standing committees
   B. Subcommittees
   C. Conference committees
   D. ✓ Ad hoc committees
   E. Interim committees

9. Which of the following bodies was created in 1949 to provide research and technical services to Texas legislators?
   A. The Legislative Budget Board
   B. The Legislative Budget Office
   C. The Legislative Audit Committee
   D. ✓ The Texas Legislative Council
   E. None of the above

10. Which of the following reforms for the Texas legislature is/are suggested by the authors of the text?
    A. Annual sessions
    B. Longer terms of office for legislators
    C. Higher salaries for legislators
    D. More legislative control over special sessions
    E. ✓ All of the above

11. In the Texas House of Representatives, bills are referred to the proper committees by the _____
    A. governor.
    B. lieutenant governor.
    C. ✓ speaker.
    D. parliamentarian.
    E. bill's sponsor.

12. Some limits are placed on the powers of the presiding officers of the Texas legislature by _____
    A. legislators.
    B. lobbyists and state administrators.
    C. the governor.
    D. the electorate.
    E. all of the above.

13. Biennial sessions have the effect of _____
    A. presenting legislators with many bills to consider in a relatively short time.
    B. providing legislators with more time to schedule hearings, hold debates, and fully analyze the bills.
    C. concentrating power in the presiding officers.
    D. both A and C.

14. The most significant power of a presiding officer of the Texas legislature is the right to _____
    A. recognize members who wish to speak before the legislature.
    B. vote in order to break a tie.
    C. serve on initiative and referendum panels.
    D. appoint members to standing committees.

15. The speaker of the House in Texas is _____
    A. elected by the members of the House of Representatives at the beginning of each session.
    B. elected by the citizens of Texas in a statewide election.
    C. determined by the seniority system.
    D. appointed by the lieutenant governor.

16. The approach taken by Lieutenant Governor Hobby was to _____
    A. let the process develop.
    B. be patient and listen to debate.
    C. be personally involved and control the process.
    D. both A and B.

17. Term limits would _____
    A.  enhance the power of speakers.
    B.  limit the speakers' influence.
    C.  limit the voter's right to select their elected officials.
    D. ✓ both B and C.

18. Senator Jane Nelson researched other states and found that the best way to pass term limits was through _____
    A.  active speakers advocating change.
    B. ✓ the initiative process.
    C.  the recall process.
    D.  legislators holding hearings and passing legislation.

19. Critics of the existing system believe that initiative and referendum would _____
    A.  empower voters.
    B.  weaken the influence of special-interest groups.
    C.  enable the passage of term limits.
    D. ✓ all of the above.


TRUE/FALSE

If the statement is true, write "T" to the left of the statement.  If the statement (or any part of the statement) is false, write "F" to the left of the statement.

20.  Every state in the United States has a bicameral legislature.

21.  The Texas legislature is responsible for its own redistricting as well as for that of the Texas congressional delegation.

22.  Compared to legislators in other large states, Texas legislators are well paid.

23.  Because all of the formal powers of the lieutenant governor and the speaker are specified by the Texas Constitution, legislators have no recourse against a presiding officer who is arbitrary in the use of power.

## ESSAY PROBLEM QUESTIONS

24. What is redistricting? Describe the process by which this function is carried out in Texas including the role of the Legislative Redistricting Board.

25. What effect has the emergence of a two-party system in the state had on the organization of the Texas legislature? Do you think the nonpartisan leadership style of House Speaker Pete Laney and Lt. Gov. Bob Bullock is likely to persist, or does the growing strength of the Republican party in Texas require Democratic leaders to adopt a more partisan stance?

26. Describe the committee system in the Texas legislature. What do the various types of committees do? Why are committees so important in the legislative process?

27. Describe the powers of the presiding officers in the Texas legislature. Explain the factors that limit them from having absolute control over the process. Are the presiding officers becoming more powerful, or have changes in the legislature and in the broader political context reduced their powers?

28. Define *initiative* and *referendum*, and assess the pros and cons that these procedures would have on the presiding officers and the legislative process. Which do you favor?

# ANSWER KEY

The following provides the answers and references for the Practice Test questions. Objectives are referenced using the following abbreviations:

T=Textbook Objectives    V=Video Objectives

| | Answer | Learning Objectives | References |
|---|---|---|---|
| 1. | D | T 1 | Kraemer, p. 163 |
| 2. | B | T 2 | Kraemer, p. 164 |
| 3. | C | T 3 | Kraemer, p. 165 |
| 4. | A | T 4 | Kraemer, p. 174 |
| 5. | D | T 5 | Kraemer, p. 174 |
| 6. | C | T 6 | Kraemer, p. 178 |
| 7. | C | T 7 | Kraemer, p. 181 |
| 8. | D | T 8 | Kraemer, p. 184 |
| 9. | D | T 9 | Kraemer, p. 187 |
| 10. | E | T 10 | Kraemer, pp. 188–190 |
| 11. | C | T 11 | Kraemer, p. 182 |
| 12. | E | T 12 | Kraemer, pp. 204–206 |
| 13. | D | V 13 | Video |
| 14. | D | V 14 | Video |
| 15. | A | V 15 | Video |
| 16. | D | V 16 | Video |
| 17. | D | V 17 | Video |
| 18. | B | V 17 | Video |
| 19. | D | V 17 | Video |
| 20. | F | T 1 | Kraemer, p. 162 |
| 21. | T | T 3 | Kraemer, p. 160 |
| 22. | F | T 5 | Kraemer, pp. 174–175 |
| 23. | F | T 12 | Kraemer, p. 205 |
| 24. | | T 3 | Kraemer, pp. 165–172 |
| 25. | | T 4 | Kraemer, pp. 180–183 |
| 26. | | T 8 | Kraemer, pp. 183–186 |
| 27. | | T12, V13, V14, V15 | Kraemer, pp. 180–183; Video |
| 28. | | V 17 | Video |

# Lesson 15

# The Legislative Process in Texas

## LESSON ASSIGNMENTS

Review the following assignments in order to schedule your time appropriately. For each lesson you will have a reading assignment and a video assignment.

Text:

>   Kraemer, et al., *Texas Politics*, Chapter 7, "The Legislative Process," pp. 194–222.

Video:

>   "The Legislative Process in Texas" from the series *Texas Politics and You*.

Activities:

>   One or more activities may be assigned to this lesson. Refer to your syllabus.

## OVERVIEW

The principal job of the Texas legislature is to make laws. While only a member of the legislature may introduce a bill directly into the legislative process, the law that is enacted is a product of many political influences and a survivor of many hurdles. Public opinion, special interest groups, and government officials all impact the creation of new laws. A firm understanding of the rules and customs of each house is required for successful passage or defeat of legislation.

## LESSON GOAL

You will describe and critique the major steps that are taken to enact legislation and constitutional amendments in Texas and assess the influence exerted by various forces involved in the political process.

# TEXTBOOK OBJECTIVES

The following objectives are designed to help you get the most from the text. Review them before reading the assignment. You may want to write notes to reinforce what you have learned.

1. Describe the three types of resolutions that can be passed in each house.

2. Describe the five steps required for a bill to become law in Texas.

3. Explain the handicaps that legislators face.

4. Explain the significance of adjusting to shifting alliances.

5. Describe the criteria used to evaluate legislative sessions.

6. Explain how the suggested reforms in the areas of committees, the leadership, and ties to lobbyists would improve the formal structure for the legislature.

7. Explain how the nonlegislators such as the governor, administrators, and courts make law.


# VIDEO OBJECTIVES

The following objectives are designed to help you get the most from the video segment of this lesson. Review them before watching the video. You may want to write notes to reinforce what you have learned.

8. Discuss House Bill 11 and steps taken by the sponsor, and assess its outcome.

9. Describe how the 1997 legislation to limit children's access to tobacco was passed; include an explanation of the function of interim studies, the Senate Health and Human Services Committee, and lobbyists.

10. Explain and assess the function of "unwritten rules" and parliamentary rules and how a competitive two-party system might impact each.

11. Use the example of "home equity" and describe and evaluate the influence of the public, lobbyists, and legislators in amending the Texas Constitution.

PRACTICE TEST

After reading the assignment, watching the video, and addressing the objectives, you should be able to complete the following Practice Test. Some essay questions in this Practice Test may be included in your exams. When you have completed the Practice Test, turn to the Answer Key to score your answers.

MULTIPLE CHOICE

Select the single best answer. If more than one answer is required, it will be so indicated.

1. Which of the following forms of legislative action is used by the Texas legislature to propose constitutional amendments?
   A. Bill
   B. Simple resolution
   C. Concurrent resolution
   D. ✓ Joint resolution
   E. None of the above

2. Which of the following types of legislation may not originate in the Texas Senate?
   A. Education bills
   B. ✓ Revenue bills
   C. Local bills
   D. Welfare bills

3. An effort to force the withdrawal of a controversial bill through the use of the unlimited privileges of debate in the Senate is called a _____
   A. cloture motion.
   B. consent decree.
   C. ✓ filibuster.
   D. gerrymander.
   E. none of the above.

4. Differences between bills passed by the House and Senate are resolved by what type of committee?
   A. Standing
   B. Select
   C. Joint
   D. ✓Conference
   E. Rules

5. The public often criticizes legislators for being unprincipled, apparently because it does not understand the role of _____ in the political system.
   A. interest groups
   B. morality
   C. ✓compromise
   D. money
   E. none of the above

6. In recent years, the legislature in Texas _____
   A. has become more rural and more Democratic.
   B. has become more alike in both Houses.
   C. has become more liberal and Republican.
   D. ✓has become more urban and more Republican.
   E. none of the above.

7. Which of the following is not among the reforms recommended for the Texas legislature by the authors of the text?
   A. Reducing the number of committees
   B. Establishing a joint budget committee
   C. Providing more professional committee staff
   D. ✓Adopting a stricter seniority rule for committee membership
   E. Curbing the influence of the lobby

8. Whose opinions have the force of law unless they are successfully challenged in court?
   A. Governor
   B. Lieutenant governor
   C. Speaker
   D. ✓Attorney general
   E. Comptroller

9. Most critical for a bill's chance of success is _____
   A. a bill that is controversial.
   B. a favorable committee assignment.
   C. a sponsor who has a political agenda.
   D. a public hearing.

10. The Senate Health and Human Services Committee _____
    A. conducted interim studies.
    B. held hearings.
    C. reported a bill to limit children's access to tobacco.
    D. all of the above.

11. The bill to limit children's access to tobacco _____
    A. generated very little publicity.
    B. had little resistance from the tobacco lobby.
    C. was wanted and lobbied for heavily by the Coalition for Tobacco-Free Kids.
    D. was killed by a filibuster.

12. The benefit of abiding by "unwritten rules" is _____
    A. name-calling without having to pay any penalties.
    B. greater independence.
    C. a certain level of mutual respect.
    D. the ability to filibuster.

13. Parliamentary procedures enable _____
    A. the speaker and lieutenant governor to control the legislative process.
    B. legislators to call for points of order if they find that bills have not been processed correctly.
    C. legislators to move bills out of unfriendly committees.
    D. both B and C.

14. Bankers and moneylenders in Texas _____
    A. were opposed to home equity loans.
    B. favored home equity loans.
    C. would not present their opinions.
    D. worked with realtors to defeat passage of any changes.

## ESSAY PROBLEM QUESTIONS

15. Describe the process by which a bill becomes a law in Texas. If you were a legislator interested in passing a bill you had introduced, whose support would you be most concerned about securing? Explain.

16. Describe criteria used to evaluate legislative sessions. Which do you consider to be the most important measure?

17. What are some of the handicaps facing members of the Texas legislature as they attempt to carry out their lawmaking function? How might changes in the powers of the presiding officers affect the ability of legislators to overcome these handicaps and to legislate more effectively?

18. What is nonlegislative lawmaking? Who does it? Are these forms of lawmaking inherently undemocratic? Why or why not?

19. Trace the legislative history of House Bill 11 from its initiation to its eventual fate. What generalizations can you conclude about the legislative process?

20. Trace the legislative history of the child anti-tobacco cause, and assess the final outcome.

21. How does an amendment to the state constitution get passed? Explain what happens at each step. As a citizen, where in this process can you influence the passage or defeat of an amendment?

# ANSWER KEY

The following provides the answers and references for the Practice Test questions. Objectives are referenced using the following abbreviations:

T=Textbook Objectives   V=Video Objectives

| | Answer | Learning Objectives | References |
|---|---|---|---|
| 1. | D | T1 | Kraemer, p. 207 |
| 2. | B | T1 | Kraemer, p. 207 |
| 3. | C | T2 | Kraemer, p. 199 |
| 4. | D | T2 | Kraemer, p. 196 |
| 5. | C | T3 | Kraemer, p. 198 |
| 6. | D | T4 | Kraemer, p. 197 |
| 7. | D | T6 | Kraemer, p. 215 |
| 8. | D | T7 | Kraemer, pp. 215–218 |
| 9. | B | V8 | Video |
| 10. | D | V9 | Video |
| 11. | C | V9 | Video |
| 12. | C | V10 | Video |
| 13. | D | V10 | Video |
| 14. | B | V11 | Video |
| 15. | | T2 | Kraemer, pp. 206–212 |
| 16. | | T5 | Kraemer, pp. 215–218 |
| 17. | | T6 | Kraemer, pp. 212–214 |
| 18. | | T7 | Kraemer, pp. 219–220 |
| 19. | | V8 | Video |
| 20. | | V9 | Video |
| 21. | | V11 | Video |

# Lesson 16

# Texas: Casework and Oversight

## LESSON ASSIGNMENTS

Review the following assignments in order to schedule your time appropriately. For each lesson you will have a reading assignment and a video assignment.

Text:

> Kraemer, et al., *Texas Politics*, Chapter 6, "Organization of the Texas Legislature," pp. 158–192.

Video:

> "Texas: Casework and Oversight" from the series *Texas Politics and You.*

Activities:

> One or more activities may be assigned to this lesson. Refer to your syllabus.

## OVERVIEW

Legislators have other functions besides making laws during the legislative session. Look at how they determine what the state's policies and priorities will be. Who does the elected official really represent? How do they decide which issues they should support? And what do legislators do when they are not in session? Casework occupies much of the legislators' time as they troubleshoot or problem-solve on behalf of their constituencies. The responsibility of agency oversight illustrates yet another function legislators fulfill.

## LESSON GOAL

You should be able to explain several factors that determine how a legislator votes, identify formal functions of legislatures, and discuss the importance of casework and legislative oversight.

## TEXTBOOK OBJECTIVES

The following objectives are designed to help you get the most from the text. Review them before reading the assignment. You may want to write notes to reinforce what you have learned.

1. Explain what legislators do in fulfilling each of the seven formal functions of legislative bodies.

2. Describe the role and significance of casework.

3. Describe ways that constituents can obtain information on legislative issues.


## VIDEO OBJECTIVES

The following objectives are designed to help you get the most from the video segment of this lesson. Review them before watching the video. You may want to write notes to reinforce what you have learned.

4. Compare and contrast Representatives Beverly Woolley and Pete Gallego, and discuss how these legislators determine who and what they will represent.

5. Explain the process and results of the casework that Representative Shapiro pursued regarding sexual offender notification laws.

6. Explain the purpose of the Joint General Investigating Committee and the role of legislative oversight and its impact on the Texas Commission on Alcohol and Drug Abuse.

PRACTICE TEST

After reading the assignment, watching the video, and addressing the objectives, you should be able to complete the following Practice Test. Some essay questions in this Practice Test may be included in your exams. When you have completed the Practice Test, turn to the Answer Key to score your answers.

MULTIPLE CHOICE

Select the single best answer. If more than one answer is required, it will be so indicated.

1. The Sunset Act of 1977 and the establishment of the Sunset Advisory Commission strengthened the process of _____
   A. legislative oversight.
   B. constitutional amendment.
   C. election administration.
   D. redistricting.
   E. judicial review.

2. In order to stay connected with his constituents, Representative Pete Gallego of Marfa _____
   A. walks his entire district in a day.
   B. listens to a variety of needs from farmers and ranchers to small-business people.
   C. personally answers every letter from his primarily white, Republican constituency.
   D. stays in his district office and waits for people to come to him.

3. The "delegate" theory of representation that expects representatives to make decisions based on what their constituents want is _____
   A. generally followed by both Representatives Gallego and Woolley.
   B. generally ignored by both Representatives Gallego and Woolley.
   C. never followed by any legislators.
   D. is always clearly agreed upon by all constituents.

4. The "trustee" role of representation is acted out when legislators in Texas try to _____
   A. follow closely the wishes of their constituents.
   B. follow closely the wishes of their political party.
   C. ✓act independently, doing what is best for Texas and the country.
   D. act independently, serving their own personal interests in office.

5. According to the provisions in the Ashley Laws, sex offenders _____
   A. must register with the police when they move into a community.
   B. will receive increased penalties for repeat offenses.
   C. will have their privacy protected.
   D. ✓ A and B only.

6. The Joint General Investigating Committee in Texas _____
   A. is responsible for addressing issues of civil or criminal activity that are charged by the Senate or House.
   B. has subpoena power.
   C. investigates the way public funds are spent.
   D. ✓all of the above.

TRUE/FALSE

If the statement is true, write "T" to the left of the statement. If the statement (or any part of the statement) is false, write "F" to the left of the statement.

7. F State legislators spend more time on casework than do members of Congress.

ESSAY PROBLEM QUESTIONS

8. What are the formal functions of legislatures? What effect does the structure and organization of the Texas legislature have on the way these functions are handled?

9. Describe an example of casework, and explain how casework, an informal function, relates to the formal function of representation.

10. Explain how the public can evaluate information contained from their legislators.

11. Explain how factors such as constituency, size of district, and theories of representation might affect the voting behavior of Representatives Woolley and Gallego.

12. Describe the role of the Joint General Investigating Committee, and explain its significance regarding administrative agencies in Texas.

## ANSWER KEY

The following provides the answers and references for the Practice Test questions. Objectives are referenced using the following abbreviations:

T=Textbook Objectives   V=Video Objectives

| | Answer | Learning Objectives | References |
|---|---|---|---|
| 1. | A | T1 | Kraemer, p. 161 |
| 2. | B | V4 | Video |
| 3. | A | V4 | Video |
| 4. | C | V4 | Video |
| 5. | D | V5 | Video |
| 6. | D | V6 | Video |
| 7. | F | T2 | Kraemer, p. 162 |
| 8. | | T1 | Kraemer, pp. 159–162 |
| 9. | | T1, T2, V2 | Kraemer, p. 162; Video |
| 10. | | T3 | Kraemer, pp. 162–163 |
| 11. | | V1 | Video |
| 12. | | V3 | Video |

# Lesson 17

# The Governor

## LESSON ASSIGNMENTS

Review the following assignments in order to schedule your time appropriately. For each lesson you will have a reading assignment and a video assignment.

Text:
> Kraemer, et al., *Texas Politics*, Chapter 8, "The Governor," pp. 224–250.

Video:
> "The Governor" from the series *Texas Politics and You.*

Activities:
> One or more activities may be assigned to this lesson. Refer to your syllabus.

## OVERVIEW

The governor's office in Texas is weak in terms of formal powers, thus personality and leadership skills are extremely important in the management of the state's multiple interests. The Texas Constitution identifies and assigns power to several other executives, such as the attorney general and the comptroller, who are also independently elected by the public to become part of the plural executive system. The gubernatorial management of the bureaucracy in Texas is further hampered by a loosely connected bureaucracy composed of many appointees who maintain their fixed terms well into succeeding governors' administrations. Still, governors today are expected to provide leadership in heading up a large bureaucracy and responding to whatever crisis or economic, social, or political problems may confront the state.

## LESSON GOAL

You should be able to describe the role of the governor in Texas politics, identify the formal and informal resources, and assess the governor's ability to influence the direction and content of public policy.

## TEXTBOOK OBJECTIVES

The following objectives are designed to help you get the most from the text. Review them before reading the assignment. You may want to write notes to reinforce what you have learned.

1. Explain why gubernatorial elections are held in the off-year to presidential elections, and discuss the impact on voter turnout.

2. Describe the procedures for gubernatorial removal and succession.

3. Describe how the governor's personal staff assists with the legislative and executive tasks.

4. List the formal qualifications and explain the significance of the personal characteristics generally needed to become governor.

5. Describe five formal roles of the governor and assess the powers of each.

6. Explain how informal roles can enhance the governor's powers.

7. Describe and assess gubernatorial leadership styles.

## VIDEO OBJECTIVES

The following objectives are designed to help you get the most from the video segment of this lesson. Review them before watching the video. You may want to write notes to reinforce what you have learned.

8. Explain why the gubernatorial office in Texas is often described as a "paper tiger" and how despite these limitations, governors can still provide strong policy leadership.

9. Evaluate how effective Governor Clements was in setting the policy agenda, affecting the formation and adoption of policies, and impacting administrative agencies.

10. Evaluate how effective Governor Richards was in setting the policy agenda, affecting the formation and adoption of policies, and impacting administrative agencies.

11. Evaluate how effective Governor Bush was in setting the policy agenda, affecting the formation and adoption of policies, and impacting administrative agencies.

## PRACTICE TEST

After reading the assignment, watching the video, and addressing the objectives, you should be able to complete the following Practice Test. Some essay questions in this Practice Test may be included in your exams. When you have completed the Practice Test, turn to the Answer Key to score your answers.

## MULTIPLE CHOICE

Select the single best answer. If more than one answer is required, it will be so indicated.

1. Since the constitutional amendment extending the governor's term of office from two years to four years went into effect, gubernatorial elections in Texas _____
   A. have always been held in the same year as presidential elections.
   B. have always seen a higher voter turnout.
   C. have always been held in the off-year from presidential elections.
   D. tend to focus more on issues and not on personalities.

2. When the governor of Texas dies, resigns, or is removed from office by impeachment and conviction, who becomes governor?
   A. Lieutenant governor
   B. Speaker of the House
   C. Attorney general
   D. Secretary of state
   E. Adjutant general

3. The Office of General Counsel and the Office of Music, Film, Television, and Multimedia Industries are both part of the _____
   A. Policy Council.
   B. Office of Budget and Planning.
   C. Office of the Governor.
   D. Commerce Department.
   E. Legislative Budget Board.

4. Which of the following is NOT one of the personal characteristics shared by most Texas governors?
   A. Politically liberal
   B. Wealthy
   C. Protestant
   D. Involved in civic affairs
   E. Male

5. Gubernatorial appointments in Texas must be confirmed by the state's _____
   A. Supreme Court.
   B. Senate.
   C. House of Representatives.
   D. secretary of state.
   E. attorney general.

6. Using the media for public appearances to gain support for programs and visiting disaster victims are aspects of the governor's role as _____
   A. chief executive.
   B. commander in chief/top cop.
   C. chief intergovernmental diplomat.
   D. chief of party.
   E. leader of the people.

7. Which of the following governors of Texas could most accurately be described as "atypical" and is known for the quality and diversity of the appointments made?
   A. Dolph Briscoe
   B. Bill Clements
   C. Mark White
   D. Ann Richards
   E. George W. Bush

8. The gubernatorial office in Texas is often described as a "paper tiger," because _____
   A. the Texas Constitution was written to limit the governor's formal powers.
   B. some see the office as a position of symbols without real teeth.
   C. the governor's range of appointments and role in the budget process is limited.
   D. ✓ all of the above.

9. Opportunities for the governor to be chief policy maker include the fact that the governor _____
   A. is the most visible officeholder.
   B. has a strong veto power.
   C. if politically skillful, can utilize the media for public relations.
   D. ✓ all of the above.

10. Governor Clements had difficulties in his first term in office because _____
   A. he had to work with a legislature that was dominated by the opposite political party.
   B. his leadership style reflected his business background.
   C. he was not familiar with legislative procedures.
   D. ✓ all of the above.

11. A leadership tool that Governor Clements found especially helpful was the _____
   A. removal power.
   B. ✓ veto power.
   C. power to call special sessions.
   D. media power.

12. An advantage that Governor Richards had over Governor Clements was her ability to _____
   A. ✓ communicate to the legislature and through the media with a sense of humor.
   B. influence policy makers with her boardroom background.
   C. use the experience she had gained while serving in the legislature.
   D. both B and C.

13. Governor Richards was successful in the policy areas of _____
    A. instituting an alcohol and drug treatment program.
    B. encouraging legislators to propose an amendment to approve of a lottery.
    C. negotiating school finance reforms.
    D. A and B only.

14. Governor Bush quickly earned a reputation for being the first governor
    to _____
    A. appoint minorities to positions of power.
    B. be a nonpartisan problem solver.
    C. be a strong party leader and an ideologue.
    D. be a figurehead.

15. Despite constitutional constraints, Governor Bush believed that he had the
    power to _____
    A. call special sessions and use the veto.
    B. appoint numerous people to serve the state.
    C. utilize press conferences to promote his goals.
    D. all of the above.

ESSAY PROBLEM QUESTIONS

16. What factors limit the Texas governor's ability to function effectively as chief
    executive? Given these limitations, how can the governor influence the
    operation of the executive branch?

17. Describe the governor's powers in the area of budgeting and planning. How
    significant are these powers? What staff resources are available to the
    governor to facilitate the exercise of these powers?

18. What formal legislative powers does the governor of Texas possess? How do
    these powers compare with the legislative powers of the president of the United
    States? Would you agree that the governor's role as chief legislator is the most
    significant role the Texas Constitution permits him or her to play? Why or why
    not?

19. What are the informal roles that the governor of Texas is expected to play? Since these roles are not constitutionally mandated, how are they derived? Of what value are these roles to the governor?

20. Based on the lessons that can be drawn from the text's biographical sketches of recent governors, describe an "ideal" Texas governor. What prior experience should he or she have? What personality characteristics and leadership style seem best suited for one who holds the office? Compare and contrast Governors Clements, Richards, and Bush in your answer.

## ANSWER KEY

The following provides the answers and references for the Practice Test questions. Objectives are referenced using the following abbreviations:

T=Textbook Objectives   V=Video Objectives

| | Answer | Learning Objectives | References |
|---|---|---|---|
| 1. | C | T 1 | Kraemer, p. 225 |
| 2. | A | T 2 | Kraemer, pp. 226–227 |
| 3. | C | T 3 | Kraemer, pp. 229–231 |
| 4. | A | T 4 | Kraemer, pp. 231–232 |
| 5. | B | T 5 | Kraemer, p. 233 |
| 6. | E | T 6 | Kraemer, pp. 234–236 |
| 7. | D | T 7 | Kraemer, p. 231 |
| 8. | D | V8 | Video |
| 9. | D | V8 | Video |
| 10. | D | V9 | Video |
| 11. | B | V9 | Video |
| 12. | A | V10 | Video |
| 13. | D | V10 | Video |
| 14. | B | V11 | Video |
| 15. | D | V11 | Kramer, p. 236; Video |
| 16. | | T 5 | Kraemer, p. 239 |
| 17. | | T 5 | Kraemer, p. 239 |
| 18. | | T 5 | Kraemer, pp. 240–243 |
| 19. | | T 6 | Kraemer, pp. 245–248 |
| 20. | | T7, V8–V11 | Kraemer, pp. 231–234; Video |

# Lesson 18

# Texas Bureaucracy

## LESSON ASSIGNMENTS

Review the following assignments in order to schedule your time appropriately. For each lesson you will have a reading assignment and a video assignment.

Text:

> Kraemer, et al., *Texas Politics*, Chapter 9, "The Administrative State," pp. 252–283.

Video:

> "Texas Bureaucracy" from the series *Texas Politics and You*.

Activities:

> One or more activities may be assigned to this lesson. Refer to your syllabus.

## OVERVIEW

Texas has a plural executive which includes the governor and several independently elected statewide officeholders. Texas relies upon an administrative system composed of agencies, boards, and commissions to carry out the day-to-day governmental functions of transforming policies enacted by elected officials into programs and services. A significant aspect of the public administrative system in Texas is the diffusion of responsibility and a concern that the bureaucracy has become too independent. Numerous efforts have been taken to simplify the administrative structure and make the agents of government more accountable.

## LESSON GOAL

You should be able to explain the role of the Texas bureaucracy and identify some techniques that have been adopted to improve the management of such an immense collection of state administrative agencies.

## TEXTBOOK OBJECTIVES

The following objectives are designed to help you get the most from the text. Review them before reading the assignment. You may want to write notes to reinforce what you have learned.

1.  Identify and explain five different types of state agencies.

2.  Compare traditional characteristics of a bureaucracy to modern bureaucracies.

3.  Explain why and how agency people seek survival.

4.  Describe how bureaucrats influence the content and meaning of policies and laws.

5.  Explain the effect of "goal displacement," and describe the five conditions that cause it.

6.  Describe how each branch of government can hold the bureaucracy accountable.

7.  Explain how the public can ensure accountability on the part of state administration.

8.  Explain why coordinating and controlling the bureaucracy in Texas is difficult.

9.  Explain how a cabinet-type government would alter the Texas administrative structure.

## VIDEO OBJECTIVES

The following objectives are designed to help you get the most from the video segment of this lesson. Review them before watching the video. You may want to write notes to reinforce what you have learned.

10.  Describe the role of the state bureaucracy, and identify areas of responsibility.

11.  Explain how members of the bureaucracy are held accountable for what they do.

12.  Discuss and assess measures that have been taken to improve the bureaucracy: the Whistle-blower Act, the Texas Performance Review and the Lone Star Card, the Sunset Commission, and the abolishment of the office of treasurer.

13.  Explain the role the bureaucracy plays in regulating the nursing home industry.

## PRACTICE TEST

After reading the assignment, watching the video, and addressing the objectives, you should be able to complete the following Practice Test. Some essay questions in this Practice Test may be included in your exams. When you have completed the Practice Test, turn to the Answer Key to score your answers.

MULTIPLE CHOICE

Select the single best answer. If more than one answer is required, it will be so indicated.

1.  The official responsible for certifying elections and maintaining records on campaign expenditures is the _____
    A.  attorney general.
    B.  treasurer.
    C.  secretary of state.
    D.  lieutenant governor.
    E.  governor.

2. Members of appointed boards and commissions _____
   A. are all appointed by the governor.
   B. serve four-year overlapping terms.
   C. serve without pay.
   D. generally have no authority to make policy.
   E. all of the above.

3. The Texas Railroad Commission is responsible for the regulation of _____
   A. campaign expenditures.
   B. the oil and gas industry.
   C. land leases.
   D. consumer protection regarding pesticides.
   E. all of the above.

4. The rise in the United States of an unpredictable boom-and-bust economy and widespread poverty resulted from the combination of a pseudo laissez-faire business philosophy and a social philosophy of _____
   A. populism.
   B. traditionalism.
   C. socialism.
   D. social Darwinism.
   E. none of the above.

5. According to Max Weber, hierarchical authority, defined jurisdictions, and extensive rules and regulations are all characteristics of _____
   A. government.
   B. politics.
   C. bureaucracy.
   D. legislatures.
   E. all of the above.

6. A modern characteristic of bureaucracies exemplified in the existence of the Sunset Law in Texas and other states is _____
   A. "red tape."
   B. uncontrolled growth.
   C. job specialization.
   D. reorganization.
   E. political neutrality.

7. The shifting of bureaucratic orientation where the public interest is forgotten and the agency's clientele groups become less regulated is known as _____
   A. performance review.
   B. goal displacement.
   C. sunshine activities.
   D. whistle-blowing.

8. What person or body reviews all statutory boards, commissions, and departments in Texas and recommends to the legislature whether or not they should be continued?
   A. Governor
   B. Lieutenant governor
   C. Sunset Advisory Commission
   D. Legislative Audit Committee
   E. Legislative Budget Board

9. Which of the following statements about the Texas bureaucracy is NOT correct?
   A. The task of carrying out the day-to-day work of government is performed in administrative agencies, boards, and commissions.
   B. Texas has a very decentralized administrative bureaucracy.
   C. Public administration is indispensable in a complex society that demands a multitude of programs and policies.
   D. Administrative units are where most citizens have the least contact with government.

10. The Health and Human Services Commissioner is _____
    A. the chief medical and health official in Texas who is responsible for integrating health and social services.
    B. the person responsible for Texas' dealing with foreign countries.
    C. the state's banker.
    D. the person responsible for regulating the use of pesticides.

11. Which of the following is NOT a factor limiting the authority of the various boards and commissions?
    A. Level of attention paid to the program by voters and media
    B. Oversight by the legislature through the budget
    C. Organizational structure with a chain of command placing the agency under the direct control of the governor
    D. Private organizations that serve as watchdogs for consumers

12. The whistle-blower story tells us that _____
    A. the bureaucracy is one of the least important arenas for political struggles.
    B. regulatory activities are immune to pressure from interest groups.
    C. individuals take substantial risks in exposing their agency or department to outside scrutiny.
    D. state agencies are sensitive to the concerns of industry.

13. The Sunset Commission has the responsibility for _____
    A. reviewing state agencies on a periodic basis to determine whether the agencies should continue.
    B. investigating citizens' complaints and filing criminal charges against government wrongdoing.
    C. reviewing all regulations before implementation to determine whether they conform with the governor's wishes.
    D. all of the above.

14. The motivation behind more regulatory policies for the nursing home industry in Texas is to _____
    A. reduce the nursing-home business' ability to make a profit.
    B. achieve such social goals as safety and health.
    C. extend government control over all aspects of daily life.
    D. pass on costs to private businesses.

TRUE/FALSE

If the statement is true, write "T" to the left of the statement. If the statement (or any part of the statement) is false, write "F" to the left of the statement.

15. The relationship between the Texas Department of Transportation and the Texas Good Roads and Transportation Association is an example of an agency-clientele relationship.

16. "Administrative discretion" refers to the ability of bureaucrats to use their own judgment as to just how laws should be carried out.

17. Bureaucrats may directly influence legislation by drafting bills, furnishing information to legislators, and lobbying.

18. The Sunset Advisory Commission is responsible for reviewing all statutory boards, commissions, and departments (except colleges and universities) on a twelve-year cycle.

19. The Texas Open Records Act is sometimes called the Sunset Law.

ESSAY PROBLEM QUESTIONS

20. What, according to Max Weber, are the characteristics of bureaucratic organization? What do the authors of the text suggest are the modern characteristics of bureaucracies? What does that mean in terms of making and implementing policy?

21. To whom are unelected bureaucrats accountable in Texas? Are the methods used by Texas to ensure bureaucratic accountability adequate? What should be done to increase bureaucratic accountability if this, in fact, is necessary?

22. What are the major state agencies with elected executives? What are the primary functions of each?

23. What changes would a cabinet-type government have on the Texas executive branch?

24. Discuss characteristics of the state administrative system, and assess the validity of the criticism that the system is too fragmented and lacks accountability.

25. Describe and assess the attempts taken by the Sunset Commission and the Texas Performance Review (Lone Star Card) to streamline the government in Texas.

26. Describe the difficulties that were faced by the residents in some nursing homes in Texas, and explain the governmental steps that were taken to improve the operating standards.

## ANSWER KEY

The following provides the answers and references for the Practice Test questions. Objectives are referenced using the following abbreviations:

T=Textbook Objectives   V=Video Objectives

| | Answer | Learning Objectives | References |
|---|---|---|---|
| 1. | C | T 1 | Kraemer, p. 258 |
| 2. | C | T 1 | Kraemer, p. 258 |
| 3. | B | T 1 | Kraemer, p. 259 |
| 4. | D | T 1 | Kraemer, p. 261 |
| 5. | C | T 2 | Kraemer, p. 265 |
| 6. | D | T 2 | Kraemer, p. 268 |
| 7. | B | T 5 | Kraemer, p. 273 |
| 8. | C | T 6 | Kraemer, pp. 277–278 |
| 9. | D | V14 | Video |
| 10. | A | V14 | Video |
| 11. | C | V15 | Video |
| 12. | C | V16 | Video |
| 13. | A | V16 | Video |
| 14. | B | V17 | Video |
| 15. | T | T 3 | Kraemer, p. 269 |
| 16. | T | T 4 | Kraemer, p. 272 |
| 17. | T | T 4 | Kraemer, pp. 272–273 |
| 18. | T | T 6 | Kraemer, p. 278 |
| 19. | F | T 7 | Kraemer, p. 279 |
| 20. | | T 2 | Kraemer, pp. 265–267 |
| 21. | | T6, T7 | Kraemer, pp. 275–281 |
| 22. | | T 9 | Kraemer, pp. 255–258 |
| 23. | | T 13 | Kraemer, pp. 275–277 |
| 24. | | V14, V15, V16, V17 | Video |
| 25. | | V16 | Video |
| 26. | | V17 | Video |

# Lesson 19

# Fiscal Policy

## LESSON ASSIGNMENTS

Review the following assignments in order to schedule your time appropriately. For each lesson you will have a reading assignment and a video assignment.

Text:

> Kraemer, et al., *Texas Politics*, Chapter 13, "The State Economy and the Financing of State Government," pp. 382–413.

Video:

> "Fiscal Policy" from the series *Texas Politics and You.*

Activities:

> One or more activities may be assigned to this lesson. Refer to your syllabus.

## OVERVIEW

Fiscal policy—the taxing and spending decisions—presents great challenges to state officials. Who will pay for the costs of government and who will not and which programs will get funded are political questions to be resolved. Historically, fiscal policy in Texas favored low taxes and low spending. The decline in oil prices, the economic downturn in the 1980s, and the attempts by Washington to cut back on funding reduced monetary resources. At the same time, there was a continuing increase in demand for spending in many areas such as education, health and human services, public safety and corrections, highways, and public transportation. State leaders are forced to reassess state responsibilities and all aspects of revenue raising and spending.

# LESSON GOAL

You should be able to describe Texas' fiscal policy and budgetary process and explain the legal and political constraints that affect the revenue and spending needs.

# TEXTBOOK OBJECTIVES

The following objectives are designed to help you get the most from the text. Review them before reading the assignment. You may want to write notes to reinforce what you have learned.

1. Explain how the economy affects the government's ability to generate needed revenue.

2. Analyze where revenue is raised in Texas.

3. Describe the role of the three officials who are most concerned with Texas' financial administration.

4. Assess the various nontax sources of revenue.

5. Describe the Texas tax system, and identify and explain how different taxing policies are either progressive or regressive.

6. Analyze the "benefit theory."

7. Describe the revenue problems of the 1980s and early 1990s.

8. Assess what the state can do to improve the general revenue structure.

9. Describe the steps involved in budget planning for government programs in Texas.

10. Explain the role of the three committees with primary responsibility for budgeting and appropriations.

11. Assess the categories of government spending, and determine how Texas compares to other states.

## VIDEO OBJECTIVES

The following objectives are designed to help you get the most from the video segment of this lesson. Review them before watching the video. You may want to write notes to reinforce what you have learned.

12. Identify the different sources of revenue — both tax and nontax sources— that Texas uses to pay for public services.

13. Explain the characteristics of a good tax system and the difference between progressive and regressive taxes, and evaluate the impact that the tax system in Texas has on different income groups.

14. Explain how public schools are financed in Texas and why some school districts initially have more money than other school districts and how this inequity is resolved.

15. Identify traditional barriers to tax reform, and assess the likelihood of passing a state personal income tax.

## PRACTICE TEST

After reading the assignment, watching the video, and addressing the objectives, you should be able to complete the following Practice Test. Some essay questions in this Practice Test may be included in your exams. When you have completed the Practice Test, turn to the Answer Key to score your answers.

MULTIPLE CHOICE

Select the single best answer. If more than one answer is required, it will be so indicated.

1. Because the tax system in Texas is not easily adjusted to ups and downs in the economy, it is said to _____
   A. be recession-driven.
   B. be inflation-driven.
   C. lack progressivity.
   D. lack regressivity.
   E. lack elasticity.

2. Which of the following categories is providing the greatest share of revenue in the Texas budget for the 2000–2001 biennium?
   A. Taxes
   B. Federal grants
   C. Fees and other sources
   D. Investment income
   E. None of the above

3. Which of the following officials serves as the state's tax collector?
   A. Attorney general
   B. Treasurer
   C. Comptroller
   D. Secretary of state
   E. Auditor

4. Which of the following types of federal grants could be used only for programs specified in the grant?
   A. Categorical grants-in-aid
   B. General revenue sharing
   C. Block grants
   D. Community development grants
   E. None of the above

5. Because framers of the state constitution believed in "pay-as-you-go" government, emergency borrowing by the state must be approved by _____
   A. a two-thirds majority vote of the legislature.
   B. a four-fifths majority vote of the legislature.
   C. the governor, the lieutenant governor, and the speaker of the House.
   D. the governor, the treasurer, and the comptroller of public accounts.
   E. the lieutenant governor, the speaker of the House, and the treasurer.

6. Which of the following types of tax does Texas NOT have?
   A. Motor fuels tax
   B. Personal income tax
   C. Excise tax
   D. General sales tax
   E. Severance tax

Lesson 19—Fiscal Policy

7. Which of the following taxes is both regulatory and revenue-producing?
   A. The general sales tax
   B. The insurance premium tax
   C. The ad valorem property tax
   D. The tobacco and alcohol tax
   E. None of the above

8. Reliance on a strict "benefit theory" of taxation would affect _____ most negatively.
   A. corporations
   B. nonprofit organizations
   C. upper-income citizens
   D. middle-income citizens
   E. lower-income citizens

9. The two state agencies that play a major role in the initial formulation of the budget are the Office of Budget and Planning and the _____
   A. Legislative Budget Board.
   B. Legislative Reference Service.
   C. General Accounting Office.
   D. Comptroller's Office.
   E. Treasurer's Office.

10. The largest single functional category of state spending in Texas is
   _____
   A. health and human services.
   B. general government.
   C. education.
   D. public safety and corrections.
   E. business and economic development.

11. The tax resource that the state of Texas derives most of its revenue from is the _____
   A. severance tax.
   B. income tax.
   C. property tax.
   D. sales tax.

12. According to Professor Newell, a good tax system is _____
    A. one that collects the money that it needs.
    B. fair, balanced, and equitable.
    C. one that relies heavily on sales tax.
    D. both A and B.

13. A constitutional amendment was approved which increased property tax exemptions from $5,000 to $15,000 per homeowner. How did this affect the Sunnyvale Independent School District?
    A. Sunnyvale was no longer classified as a wealthy school district.
    B. Sunnyvale was no longer classified as a poor school district.
    C. Sunnyvale decided to increase the tax rate in their district.
    D. Sunnyvale closed its schools.

14. Critics of adding a personal income tax in Texas claim that _____
    A. people do not like the idea and will not vote to approve it.
    B. it would be difficult to collect and enforce.
    C. it would require a large bureaucracy.
    D. all of the above.


TRUE/FALSE

If the statement is true, write "T" to the left of the statement. If the statement (or any part of the statement) is false, write "F" to the left of the statement.

15. Between 1971 and 1984, there were no increases in state tax rates and no new taxes adopted in Texas.

16. The three committees of the legislature with primary responsibility for budgeting and appropriating are the House Ways and Means Committee, the House Appropriations Committee, and the Senate Finance Committee.

## ESSAY PROBLEM QUESTIONS

17. Explain why the 1970s was a period of budgetary growth while the 1980s and 1990s has been a period of construction.

18. What is the difference between a progressive and a regressive system of taxation? How would you characterize Texas' tax system? What changes, if any, would you recommend be made in Texas' system in order to improve it from the standpoint of fairness?

19. Why has Texas had problems generating adequate revenues to support state programs in recent years? What has been the state's typical response to the problem of revenue shortfalls? What would you recommend be done in order to avert future revenue problems?

20. What are the chances that Texas will adopt a personal income tax in the near future? How do you explain the state's reluctance to consider an income tax? What factors might make the adoption of an income tax more likely now than in the past?

21. Describe the process of budgeting and appropriating funds for government programs in Texas. What are the advantages and disadvantages of the dual-budgeting system as it operates in Texas?

# ANSWER KEY

The following provides the answers and references for the Practice Test questions. Objectives are referenced using the following abbreviations:

T=Textbook Objectives   V=Video Objectives

| | Answer | Learning Objectives | References |
|---|---|---|---|
| 1. | E | T 1 | Kraemer, pp. 386–387 |
| 2. | A | T 2 | Kraemer, p. 388 |
| 3. | C | T 3 | Kraemer, pp. 256–257 |
| 4. | A | T 4 | Kraemer, pp. 390–391 |
| 5. | B | T 4 | Kraemer, p. 392 |
| 6. | B | T 5 | Kraemer, p. 389 |
| 7. | D | T 5 | Kraemer, p. 393 |
| 8. | E | T 6 | Kraemer, p. 398 |
| 9. | A | T 9 | Kraemer, pp. 405–406 |
| 10. | C | T 11 | Kraemer, p. 408 |
| 11. | D | V12 | Video |
| 12. | D | V13 | Video |
| 13. | A | V14 | Video |
| 14. | D | V15 | Video |
| 15. | T | T 7 | Kraemer, p. 399 |
| 16. | T | T 10 | Kraemer, p. 406 |
| 17. | | T 1 | Kraemer, pp. 399–404 |
| 18. | | T5, V13 | Kraemer, pp. 394–394; Video |
| 19. | | T7, T8 | Kraemer, pp. 399–402 |
| 20. | | T8, V15 | Kraemer, pp. 394–404; Video |
| 21. | | T 9 | Kraemer, pp. 405–411 |

# Lesson 20

# Globalism: NAFTA and Texas

## LESSON ASSIGNMENTS

Review the following assignments in order to schedule your time appropriately. For each lesson you will have a reading assignment and a video assignment.

Text:

> Kraemer, et al., *Texas Politics*, Chapter 15, "The Future of Texas Politics," pp. 446–452.

Video:

> "Globalism: NAFTA and Texas" from the series *Texas Politics and You.*

Activities:

> One or more activities may be assigned to this lesson. Refer to your syllabus.

## OVERVIEW

The economy is an important issue for everyone in the state of Texas. Recruiting new industries and expanding markets for agricultural products and manufacturing affect jobs, savings and loans, real estate, and construction. In 1987, the Texas legislature created the Texas Department of Commerce to help promote commerce and economic development. Subsequent trade offices have been established to promote Texas products and Texas companies and solicit relocation of foreign businesses to Texas. In 1997, the Texas Department of Commerce was renamed the Texas Department of Economic Development.

The North American Free Trade Agreement (NAFTA) was adopted in 1993 by the national government to promote economic development and is especially important for Texas and its neighbor, Mexico. The increased economic integration with Mexico has resulted in discussion of issues such as the environment, education, and tourism.

---

Economic changes bring about political changes; historically, those who embraced the traditional Texas culture and values preferred limited governmental involvement with the market forces. However, with the renewed interest in economic diversification and transformation, we see public officials actively developing policies to benefit and attract new businesses and new industries. These social and economic changes will likely affect the political arena in Texas as new interest groups and new powers emerge.

## LESSON GOAL

You should be able to understand how NAFTA impacts the globalization of Texas and assess the programs and policies that attempt to ensure economic growth.

## TEXTBOOK OBJECTIVES

The following objectives are designed to help you get the most from the text. Review them before reading the assignment. You may want to write notes to reinforce what you have learned.

1. Describe the economic climate in Texas in the 1990s.

2. Assess the strategies that are recommended for Texas to prosper in the global market of the twenty-first century.

## VIDEO OBJECTIVES

The following objectives are designed to help you get the most from the video segment of this lesson. Review them before watching the video. You may want to write notes to reinforce what you have learned.

3. Explain how the economy of today is fundamentally different from the economy of the past and the implications of these differences for the role of the government and businesses.

4. Assess the claim that the North American Free Trade Agreement will bring about greater demand for Texas goods and therefore will boost the economy.

5. Assess the criticism that NAFTA will lead to loss of jobs and degradation of the environment.

6. Describe the purpose of the Free Trade Alliance.

## PRACTICE TEST

After reading the assignment, watching the video, and addressing the objectives, you should be able to complete the following Practice Test. Some essay questions in this Practice Test may be included in your exams. When you have completed the Practice Test, turn to the Answer Key to score your answers.

MULTIPLE CHOICE

Select the single best answer. If more than one answer is required, it will be so indicated.

1. Which of the following statements regarding the significance of oil and gas in the Texas economy is correct?
   A. Oil and gas currently contribute over half of the state's gross domestic product.
   B. Oil and gas currently contribute a third of the state's gross domestic product.
   C. Oil and gas currently contribute a negligible share of the state's gross domestic product.
   D. The significance of oil and gas to the state's economy is steadily diminishing.
   E. The significance of oil and gas to the state's economy has always been overestimated.

2. If Robert Reich's prediction concerning the globalization of the labor market is correct, the key to creating a prosperous Texas in the twenty-first century will be _____
   A. immigration reform.
   B. lower taxes.
   C. government-financed business incentives.
   D. strong labor unions.
   E. education.

3. The economic environment in Texas _____
   A. has shifted away from agriculture and oil to more diverse manufacturing and high-tech industries.
   B. primarily relies on oil and banking.
   C. is noted for continuing an independence from other countries because of its steady income from oil and gas.
   D. is increasingly becoming more isolated and economically backward.

4. The North American Free Trade Agreement is designed to _____
   A. create a free-trade zone at certain times of the year between Texas and Mexico.
   B. remove import tariffs and other trade barriers between the United States, Canada, and Mexico.
   C. create more low-wage jobs in U.S. border counties.
   D. help the United States import more goods than it exports.

5. The maquila industry _____
   A. provides a worker with only minimum wages.
   B. offers medical and food services in addition to salaries.
   C. is an assembly-line industry with regimented work conditions.
   D. all of the above.

6. Environmental concerns in the border region _____
   A. will require a treaty negotiation.
   B. are being addressed by the Border Environmental Cooperation Commission.
   C. will be addressed by new wastewater treatment plants.
   D. both B and C.

7. The inland port concept that the Free Trade Alliance is promoting is a way to utilize the resources in San Antonio _____
   A. to facilitate manufacturing and delivery systems between Mexico and the United States.
   B. to bring businesses together in a trade zone.
   C. to keep the monies and businesses in the United States.
   D. A and B only.

## ESSAY PROBLEM QUESTIONS

8. How has the Texas economy changed in the past twenty years?  What impact have these changes had on politics in the state?  What must the state do in order to adapt to these economic changes and those that are yet to come?

9. Assess the economic impact of NAFTA on Texas.

## ANSWER KEY

The following provides the answers and references for the Practice Test questions. Objectives are referenced using the following abbreviations:

T=Textbook Objectives   V=Video Objectives

| | Answer | Learning Objectives | References |
|---|---|---|---|
| 1. | D | T1 | Kraemer, p. 450 |
| 2. | E | T2 | Kraemer, pp. 451–452 |
| 3. | A | V3 | Video |
| 4. | B | V4 | Video |
| 5. | D | V5 | Video |
| 6. | D | V5 | Video |
| 7. | D | V6 | Video |
| 8. | | T1, T2 | Kraemer, pp. 446–459 |
| 9. | | V1, V2, V3, V4 | Video |

# Lesson 21

# The Texas Courts and the Criminal Justice System

## LESSON ASSIGNMENTS

Review the following assignments in order to schedule your time appropriately. For each lesson you will have a reading assignment and a video assignment.

Text:

Kraemer, et al., *Texas Politics*, Chapter 10, "The Judiciary," pp. 285–312, and Chapter 11, "The Substance of Justice," pp. 314–341.

Video:

"The Texas Courts and the Criminal Justice System" from the series *Texas Politics and You.*

Activities:

One or more activities may be assigned to this lesson. Refer to your syllabus.

## OVERVIEW

The courts are a very important part of the political process in Texas. There is an elaborate structure that partly explains the nature and problems of the judicial process. Reforms have been suggested. However, even if the Texas court system was perfectly organized, the level of crime and the capacity of the prisons affect the administration of justice. Texas has a vast criminal justice system that, in addition to the more than 2,500 state, county, and municipal courts, has over 1,200 different law enforcement agencies, a separate juvenile justice system, and many local probation departments. The legislature has given the Texas Department of Criminal Justice (TDCJ) the responsibility for the confinement, development of probation, and rehabilitation of felons. Two other divisions within the TDCJ are the Pardon and Paroles Division and the Community Justice Assistance Division. TDCJ is administered by the Texas Board of Criminal Justice, whose nine members are appointed by the governor with Senate approval. The case of *Ruiz v. Estelle*, which found the state liable for unconstitutional conditions in the Texas prison system, forced the state to make reforms and continues to be of importance to the administration of justice in Texas.

## LESSON GOAL

You should be able to describe the organization of the state and local judiciary in Texas and analyze the system in terms of the administration of justice.

## TEXTBOOK OBJECTIVES

The following objectives are designed to help you get the most from the text. Review them before reading the assignment. You may want to write notes to reinforce what you have learned.

1. Describe why the courts and the system of justice in Texas are in a state of crisis.

2. Explain why it is unrealistic to expect judges to be nonpolitical.

3. Describe briefly the organization, functions, and jurisdictions of the Texas judiciary, and assess whether there is a need to streamline the court system.

4. Explain how the courts are affected by the criminal element.

5. Describe the roles of the attorney general, lawyers, the state bar, and judges in the system of justice.

6. Explain the procedures for removing and reprimanding lawyers and judges.

7. Explain how the grand jury differs from the petit jury, and assess whether the processes ensure fair trials.

8. Describe the typical criminal and crime in Texas.

9. Explain the difference between blue-collar and white-collar crime.

10. Describe the civil rights for those in custody, and assess the record in Texas.

## VIDEO OBJECTIVES

The following objectives are designed to help you get the most from the video segment of this lesson. Review them before watching the video. You may want to write notes to reinforce what you have learned.

11. Explain the function and role of the Texas Department of Criminal Justice (TDCJ), and identify the purposes for confinement of convicted criminals.

12. Explain the reasons for the increase in the prison population and what Texas is doing in response to high crime, overloaded court dockets, and overcrowded prisons.

13. Explain the significance of *Ruiz v. Estelle* to Texas.

14. Identify programs in the Texas criminal justice system that are designed to reduce the likelihood that offenders will repeat their crimes.


## PRACTICE TEST

After reading the assignment, watching the video, and addressing the objectives, you should be able to complete the following Practice Test. Some essay questions in this Practice Test may be included in your exams. When you have completed the Practice Test, turn to the Answer Key to score your answers.

MULTIPLE CHOICE

Select the single best answer. If more than one answer is required, it will be so indicated.

1. The mythical vision most Americans hold of judges sees them as all of the following EXCEPT _____
   A. wise.
   B. passionate.
   C. objective.
   D. impartial.
   E. nonpolitical.

2. Which of the following are NOT part of the Texas judicial system?
   A. Municipal courts
   B. Justice of the peace courts
   C. County courts
   D. Commissioner's courts
   E. District courts

3. Which of the following Texas courts deal mainly with violations of traffic laws?
   A. Municipal courts
   B. Justice of the peace courts
   C. County courts at law
   D. Constitutional county courts
   E. District courts

4. In Texas, the principal trial court(s) for both civil and criminal cases is/are the _____
   A. municipal courts.
   B. justice of the peace courts.
   C. district courts.
   D. Supreme Court.
   E. Court of Criminal Appeals.

5. Courts of appeals in Texas do not have jurisdiction over _____
   A. civil cases appealed from district courts.
   B. criminal cases questioning the constitutionality of a statute.
   C. criminal cases involving a fine of more than $100.
   D. criminal cases involving imprisonment.
   E. criminal cases involving capital murder.

6. District court judges in Texas may be removed from office by impeachment, by action of the Texas Supreme Court, or by the governor after _____
   A. a recall election.
   B. a ruling by the Commission on Judicial Conduct.
   C. a simple majority vote of the legislature.
   D. a two-thirds majority vote of the legislature.
   E. none of the above.

7. To be qualified to serve on a jury in Texas, one must _____
   A. be a citizen of the county.
   B. be a qualified voter.
   C. be able to read and write.
   D. be neither convicted of nor under indictment for a felony.
   E. all of the above.

8. In Texas, an individual is automatically exempt from jury duty if he or she is _____
   A. a public school teacher.
   B. fifty years of age or older.
   C. a parent of teenage children.
   D. a full-time student.
   E. a government employee.

9. Although the overall crime rate in Texas has dropped in recent years, the number of violent crimes committed by _____ has increased dramatically.
   A. Anglo males
   B. Anglo females
   C. Mexican American females
   D. African American females
   E. juveniles

10. Which of the following would be considered a white-collar crime?
    A. Burglary
    B. Auto theft
    C. Assault
    D. Embezzlement
    E. All of the above

11. In the case of *Ruiz v. Estelle*, a federal court found the Texas Department of Corrections (TDC) _____
    A. guilty of cruel and unusual punishment in the administration of the state's prison system.
    B. in violation of U.S. obligation under international human rights treaties.
    C. in compliance with maximum standards measured by the Bill of Rights.
    D. none of the above.

12. Which of the following is NOT a stated purpose for the confinement of persons convicted of crimes?
    A. Isolation of criminals so that the life and property of others in society may be protected
    B. Use of the proceeds from convict labor to compensate victims for injuries they have suffered
    C. Deterrence of others from committing criminal acts
    D. Rehabilitation of convicts in order that they might become law-abiding

13. Texas has dealt with overcrowding in county jails and state prisons by _____
    A. decriminalizing many offenses.
    B. releasing prisoners early and building new prisons.
    C. contracting with other states to hold Texas inmates.
    D. all of the above.

14. *Ruiz v. Estelle* (1980) held that _____
    A. capital punishment was unconstitutional.
    B. the state was not required to fund the habeas corpus appeal of a capital felon to federal court.
    C. Texas prisons were overcrowded and characterized by conditions that violated the U.S. Constitution.
    D. privately operated prisons were unconstitutional.

15. Innovative measures that have been taken by parole offices in the Dallas region include _____
    A. job fairs.
    B. specialized programs to help build self-esteem.
    C. longer visits with family members and the parolee.
    D. all of the above.

## TRUE/FALSE

If the statement is true, write "T" to the left of the statement. If the statement (or any part of the statement) is false, write "F" to the left of the statement.

16. Justices of the peace are elected by the voters of separate precincts to four-year terms.

17. Because they avoid the uncertainties of a jury trial, plea bargains serve the cause of justice by ensuring that criminals will face punishments commensurate with their crimes.

18. Although it is not required, most lawyers in Texas maintain membership in the State Bar.

## ESSAY PROBLEM QUESTIONS

19. What reforms would you recommend in order to improve the structure of the court system in Texas?

20. What are the responsibilities of the Texas Supreme Court? How is the Supreme Court affected by (1) the division of civil and criminal jurisdiction at the highest level of the Texas judiciary and (2) the unusual scope of the Texas attorney general's responsibilities?

21. Assess the impact that *Ruiz v. Estelle* has had on the Texas Department of Criminal Justice and the lawmakers in Texas.

22. What are the problems facing the criminal justice system in Texas? Discuss possible solutions to some of these problems.

# ANSWER KEY

The following provides the answers and references for the Practice Test questions. Objectives are referenced using the following abbreviations:

T=Textbook Objectives   V=Video Objectives

| | Answer | Learning Objectives | References |
|---|---|---|---|
| 1. | B | T 2 | Kraemer, pp. 285–286 |
| 2. | D | T 3 | Kraemer, pp. 290–295, Figure 10-1 |
| 3. | A | T 3 | Kraemer, p. 292 |
| 4. | C | T 3 | Kraemer, p. 293 |
| 5. | E | T 3 | Kraemer, pp. 293–294 |
| 6. | D | T 6 | Kraemer, pp. 296–297 |
| 7. | E | T 7 | Kraemer, pp. 295–296 |
| 8. | D | T 7 | Kraemer, pp. 295–296 |
| 9. | E | T 8 | Kraemer, p. 298 |
| 10. | D | T 9 | Kraemer, pp. 297–299 |
| 11. | A | T 10 | Kraemer, pp. 331–332 |
| 12. | B | V11 | Video |
| 13. | B | V12 | Video |
| 14. | C | V13 | Video |
| 15. | D | V14 | Video |
| 16. | T | T 3 | Kraemer, p. 292 |
| 17. | F | T 4 | Kraemer, pp. 307–308 |
| 18. | F | T 5 | Kraemer, p. 290 |
| 19. | | T 1 | Kraemer, pp. 290–295 |
| 20. | | T 3 | Kraemer, pp. 294–295 |
| 21. | | T10, V13 | Kraemer, pp. 331–332, Video |
| 22. | | V11, V12, V13, V14 | Video |

# Lesson 22

# Judicial Selection in Texas

## LESSON ASSIGNMENTS

Review the following assignments in order to schedule your time appropriately. For each lesson you will have a reading assignment and a video assignment.

Text:

> Kraemer, et al., *Texas Politics*, Chapter 10, "The Judiciary," pp. 297–308.

Video:

> "Judicial Selection in Texas" from the series *Texas Politics and You.*

Activities:

> One or more activities may be assigned to this lesson. Refer to your syllabus.

## OVERVIEW

All judges in Texas, except municipal judges, are elected in partisan elections with trial court judges serving four-year terms and appellate judges serving six-year terms. Campaign contributions from law firms and special interests who are likely to be in the courts, along with low voter knowledge of judicial candidates, have raised questions and criticism of the selection process. Also, lawsuits have challenged that the at-large rather than single-member districts limit the prospects of minorities becoming judges. The League of United Latin American Citizens (LULAC) challenged the countywide election of state trial judges, but the Supreme Court in 1994 ruled that there was not enough evidence to prove that the absence of minorities on the courts was the result of an at-large system. Various judicial selection reforms have been suggested, but none have been successful. Reform has been difficult to accomplish because of competing differences in partisan goals and concerns.

# LESSON GOAL

You should be able to describe and analyze the judicial selection process in Texas and evaluate proposals for reform.

# TEXTBOOK OBJECTIVES

The following objectives are designed to help you get the most from the text. Review them before reading the assignment. You may want to write notes to reinforce what you have learned.

1. Assess the six methods that are used in the United States to select judges.

2. Explain the criticism that the selection process in Texas permits judges to be corrupted by campaign contributions.

3. Explain why the use of partisan elections is considered by some to be problematic.

4. Assess whether at-large or district elections should be held to select county judges.

5. Explain how politics affect the judicial selection process.

# VIDEO OBJECTIVES

The following objectives are designed to help you get the most from the video segment of this lesson. Review them before watching the video. You may want to write notes to reinforce what you have learned.

6. Discuss the advantages and disadvantages of a partisan elective system for judicial selection.

7. Assess the alternatives to partisan judicial elections, such as a merit plan with retention elections.

8. Discuss the conflict that minorities have had with at-large districts for judicial selection, and identify the change that minorities believe would provide for greater representation.

## PRACTICE TEST

After reading the assignment, watching the video, and addressing the objectives, you should be able to complete the following Practice Test. Some essay questions in this Practice Test may be included in your exams. When you have completed the Practice Test, turn to the Answer Key to score your answers.

MULTIPLE CHOICE

Select the single best answer. If more than one answer is required, it will be so indicated.

1. Critics of the judicial selection process in Texas complain that _____
   A. judges' reliance on campaign contributions compromise their independence.
   B. partisan elections create a divided and nonneutral judiciary.
   C. at-large elections discriminate against minorities.
   D. partisan elections may produce judges with marginal qualifications.
   E. all of the above.

2. In 1988, the League of United Latin American Citizens (LULAC) filed suit in federal court in an effort to change Texas' system of electing _____ at large.
   A. county commissioners
   B. county judges
   C. state senators
   D. state district court judges
   E. state Board of Education members

3. One analyst, James Harrington, sees the partisan election system as an advantage because _____

   A. it forces judges to come out and talk to people.
   B. it forces judges to at least identify with a political party and reveal something about themselves.
   C. it forces judges to create a political agenda and be accountable to a political party position.
   D. A and B only.

4. A major disadvantage to a partisan elective system for selection of judges is _____

   A. expensive campaign costs.
   B. low voter awareness.
   C. the perceived influence of donations from law firms and corporations.
   D. all of the above.

5. The advantage of a merit system is that it _____

   A. protects against partisan sweeps and encourages voters to consider each judge's qualifications.
   B. lowers reelection costs in money for incumbent judges and justices.
   C. takes less time and energy for judges to spend on campaigning and fund-raising.
   D. all of the above.

6. According to the Judicial Taskforce of the League of Women Voters, the best system for gaining representation in the judiciary for women and minorities is _____

   A. the current partisan election system.
   B. gubernatorial appointments.
   C. countywide partisan elections.
   D. statewide partisan elections.

## TRUE/FALSE

If the statement is true, write "T" to the left of the statement. If the statement (or any part of the statement) is false, write "F" to the left of the statement.

7. The Texas judicial system's reputation was significantly tarnished by the large campaign contributions given by attorneys for both sides in Pennzoil's $11 billion lawsuit against Texaco.

8. The 1995 legislature failed to adopt the judicial reform plan recommended by the bipartisan commission chaired by Lt. Gov. Bob Bullock in part because of Gov. George W. Bush's expressed preference for partisan elections.


## ESSAY PROBLEM QUESTIONS

9. What, in your opinion, is the best method of selecting judges in a state court system? What makes this method of selection superior to the alternatives? How would you assess the current prospects of adopting a different method of judicial selection in Texas?

10. What are the typical effects of at-large elections on minority representation? Should state county court judges be required to run for election from single-member districts, or should the at-large system be retained?

11. Is it important that the public know whether the judge is a Republican or a Democrat? Why or why not? How do judicial election campaigns strengthen the judiciary? Weaken the judiciary?

# ANSWER KEY

The following provides the answers and references for the Practice Test questions. Objectives are referenced using the following abbreviations:

T=Textbook Objectives   V=Video Objectives

| | Answer | Learning Objectives | References |
|---|---|---|---|
| 1. | B | T 2 | Kraemer, pp. 286–288 |
| 2. | B | T 4 | Kraemer, p. 287 |
| 3. | D | V 6 | Video |
| 4. | D | V 6 | Video |
| 5. | D | V 7 | Video |
| 6. | B | V 8 | Video |
| 7. | T | T 2 | Kraemer, pp. 302–303 |
| 8. | T | T 5 | Kraemer, pp. 299–301 |
| 9. | | T1, T3, T5, V6 , V7, V8 | Kraemer, pp. 286–288; Video |
| 10. | | T4, V8 | Kraemer, pp. 304–305; Video |
| 11. | | V6 | Video |

# Lesson 23

# Decision Making by the Courts

## LESSON ASSIGNMENTS

Review the following assignments in order to schedule your time appropriately. For each lesson you will have a reading assignment and a video assignment.

Text:

Kraemer, et al., *Texas Politics*, Chapter 11, "The Substance of Justice," pp. 314–341.

Video:

"Decision Making by the Courts" from the series *Texas Politics and You*.

Activities:

One or more activities may be assigned to this lesson. Refer to your syllabus.

## OVERVIEW

Courts at the national and state levels deal with a great range of questions concerning the rights and liberties of individuals and groups. The Bill of Rights limits the national government, and with the use of the Fourteenth Amendment, the process of "incorporation" helps ensure that the U.S. Constitution protects the rights of individuals and minorities against the actions of the state and local governments. Most of our constitutional history is of the U.S. Supreme Court and its role in protecting liberties; state courts have historically had a harder time establishing civil liberty protections, but that is changing. The involvement of the U.S. Supreme Court is explored through the lens of *Roe v. Wade*, which has become one of the most controversial and contentious Supreme Court cases of all time.

# LESSON GOAL

You should be able to explain why the protection and exercise of civil liberties is essential to a representative democracy and assess how federal and state court rulings affect Texas and its people.

# TEXTBOOK OBJECTIVES

The following objectives are designed to help you get the most from the text. Review them before reading the assignment. You may want to write notes to reinforce what you have learned.

1. Define *civil liberties*, and explain how individuals are protected from state and national governmental interference.

2. Explain why freedom of expression is important in a democracy, and assess the roles of U.S. and Texas courts.

3. Explain the U.S. Supreme Court's interpretation of the Second Amendment to the U.S. Constitution.

4. Describe the legal history of abortions.

5. Describe the debate between pro-choice and pro-life forces and the significance this has on the abortion issues.

6. Describe the U.S. and state court's roles in Vidor, Texas, in regard to protecting civil rights and liberties for minorities and even the Ku Klux Klan.

# VIDEO OBJECTIVES

The following objectives are designed to help you get the most from the video segment of this lesson. Review them before watching the video. You may want to write notes to reinforce what you have learned.

7. Discuss the purpose of the U.S. Bill of Rights, the Fourteenth Amendment, the Texas Bill of Rights, and the role courts play in preserving civil liberties.

8. Explain why the Texas Court of Criminal Appeals held that Texas could not tax drug dealers as well as prosecute them for illegal activities.

9. Explain why the Texas Supreme Court ruled in favor of the Ku Klux Klan.

10. Explain why the Supreme Court in *Roe v. Wade* declared Texas' law forbidding abortions unconstitutional and why the decision is categorized as an example of judicial activism.

## PRACTICE TEST

After reading the assignment, watching the video, and addressing the objectives, you should be able to complete the following Practice Test. Some essay questions in this Practice Test may be included in your exams. When you have completed the Practice Test, turn to the Answer Key to score your answers.

### MULTIPLE CHOICE

Select the single best answer. If more than one answer is required, it will be so indicated.

1. The First Amendment to the U.S. Constitution explicitly guarantees all of the following EXCEPT _____
   A. freedom of speech.
   B. freedom of the press.
   C. freedom to assemble peaceably.
   D. freedom to form political associations.
   E. freedom to petition the government for redress of grievances.

2. The National Rifle Association argues that there is a constitutional right to keep and bear arms based on the _____
   A. First Amendment.
   B. Second Amendment.
   C. Third Amendment.
   D. Fourth Amendment.
   E. Fifth Amendment.

3. Which of the following statements regarding abortion is NOT correct?
   A. Between 1860 and 1890, almost all states enacted laws to discourage or ban abortion.
   B. The Supreme Court's decision in *Roe v. Wade* was based on the right to privacy.
   C. *Roe v. Wade* made abortion a far less controversial issue in the U.S. than it had been.
   D. The Texas Republican Party included a hard-line antiabortion plank in its 1994 platform.
   E. The 1995 legislature generally ignored the issue of abortion.

4. The national government is limited in denying certain fundamental rights and liberties by _____
   A. the U.S. Bill of Rights.
   B. the Fourteenth Amendment.
   C. state Bills of Rights.
   D. all of the above.

5. State governments are limited in denying certain fundamental rights and liberties by _____
   A. the U.S. Bill of Rights and the Fourteenth Amendment.
   B. state Bills of Rights.
   C. the U.S. Bill of Rights only.
   D. both A and B.

6. In 1996, the Texas Court of Criminal Appeals ruled that prosecutors must decide whether they want drug dealers to do time or pay taxes. They cannot do both because the state's "drug tax" _____
   A. is designed to punish.
   B. is designed to produce revenue.
   C. is in violation of the constitutional protection against double jeopardy.
   D. both A and C.

7. In 1973, in *Roe v. Wade*, the Supreme Court struck down a Texas statute that allowed abortion only in cases where the mother's life was in danger. In doing so, the court _____
   A. limited the power of Texas and other states to regulate abortion.
   B. recognized a woman's "right to privacy."
   C. illustrated the judicial power to impose limitation on the state's power to regulate civil liberties.
   D. all of the above.

TRUE/FALSE

If the statement is true, write "T" to the left of the statement. If the statement (or any part of the statement) is false, write "F" to the left of the statement.

8. The right to freedom of speech is included in the category of civil liberties.

9. The U.S. Supreme Court has determined that state laws prohibiting flag burning as a form of political protest do not violate the First Amendment.

10. Unlike the Texas statute struck down in the case of *Texas v. Johnson*, the Federal Flag Protection Act of 1989 was not considered unconstitutional.

ESSAY PROBLEM QUESTIONS

11. What role do civil liberties play in supporting democratic government? What principles would you recommend be used in an effort to draw the line separating majority rule from individual rights?

12. What general lessons can be drawn concerning civil rights in Texas from the text's account of the effort to desegregate public housing in Vidor and the death of James Byrd Jr. in Jasper?

13. Discuss the role of the state and federal courts as they attempt to balance order and civil liberties, and explain and evaluate the appropriateness of judicial activism or judicial restraint. Must the rights of the "worst" of us be defended in order to protect the "best" of us?

# ANSWER KEY

The following provides the answers and references for the Practice Test questions.
Objectives are referenced using the following abbreviations:

## T=Textbook Objectives   V=Video Objectives

| | Answer | Learning Objectives | References |
|---|---|---|---|
| 1. | D | T 2 | Kraemer, p. 315 |
| 2. | B | T 3 | Kraemer, p. 322 |
| 3. | C | T 5 | Kraemer, p. 323 |
| 4. | A | V 7 | Video |
| 5. | D | V 7 | Video |
| 6. | D | V 8 | Video |
| 7. | D | V 10 | Video |
| 8. | T | T 1 | Kraemer, p. 315 |
| 9. | F | T1, T2 | Kraemer, p. 316 |
| 10. | F | T1, T2 | Kraemer, pp. 316–317 |
| 11. | | T1, T2 | Kraemer, pp. 315–320 |
| 12. | | T 6 | Kraemer, pp. 328–331 |
| 13. | | V7, V8, V9, V10 | Video |

# Lesson 24

# First Amendment Civil Liberties

## LESSON ASSIGNMENTS

Review the following assignments in order to schedule your time appropriately. For each lesson you will have a reading assignment and a video assignment.

Text:

> Kraemer, et al., *Texas Politics*, Chapter 11, "The Substance of Justice," pp. 315–321.

Video:

> "First Amendment Civil Liberties" from the series *Texas Politics and You.*

Activities:

> One or more activities may be assigned to this lesson. Refer to your syllabus.

## OVERVIEW

Courts face many dilemmas when asked to interpret the meaning of free speech and press. Do constitutional guarantees protect those who want to spout racial propaganda on local cable TV access programs? Are those who want to publicly burn an American flag protected? The limits of free speech in the United States and Texas and the conflicts between the right to free speech and other liberties are explored. Guarantees of religious freedoms are also examined through interpretations of the establishment clause and the free exercise clause.

# LESSON GOAL

You should be able to explain some of the difficulties and dilemmas that Texas faces in balancing order and protecting civil liberties in the areas of freedom of expression and religion.

# TEXTBOOK OBJECTIVES

The following objectives are designed to help you get the most from the text. Review them before reading the assignment. You may want to write notes to reinforce what you have learned.

1. Explain the dilemma judges face when interpreting the meaning of freedom of speech and press.

2. Explain the two interpretations given to the establishment clause.

3. Explain how the free exercise of religion is not an absolute right.

4. Explain why the Supreme Court has ruled that school-sponsored prayers and a state program providing for voluntary prayers is unconstitutional.

# VIDEO OBJECTIVES

The following objectives are designed to help you get the most from the video segment of this lesson. Review them before watching the video. You may want to write notes to reinforce what you have learned.

5. Describe the freedoms protected by the First Amendment, and explain how individuals maintain these freedoms without being unduly denied by state governments.

6. Explain the significance of the "clear and present danger" test to free speech.

7. Define *prior restraint* and explain how Judge Drago dealt with the issue of the airing of the TV movie of the two military cadets who would soon be on trial and the defendants' right to a fair trial.

8. Discuss the constitutional guidelines that govern anti-stalking legislation.

9. Compare and contrast the American Civil Liberties Union and the Liberty Legal Institute as they seek to protect religious rights under the Constitution.

## PRACTICE TEST

After reading the assignment, watching the video, and addressing the objectives, you should be able to complete the following Practice Test. Some essay questions in this Practice Test may be included in your exams. When you have completed the Practice Test, turn to the Answer Key to score your answers.

MULTIPLE CHOICE

Select the single best answer. If more than one answer is required, it will be so indicated.

1. The concept of a "wall of separation" is related to the First Amendment guarantee of _____
   A. freedom of speech.
   B. freedom of press.
   C. freedom of religion.
   D. the right to petition the government.
   E. none of the above.

2. Individuals are protected from wrongful state governmental actions due to the Supreme Court's interpretation that the U.S. Bill of Rights _____
   A. was always intended to limit both the Congress and the states.
   B. and the Fourteenth Amendment work together to limit the states.
   C. limits the Congress, and the state constitutions must be relied on to limit each state.
   D. is absolute and no government can regulate them.

3. Prior restraint, established in the *Near v. Minnesota* decision, is a standard that applies to questions of _____
   A. prohibiting someone from yelling "fire" in a theater.
   B. stopping the press from printing or publicly producing something.
   C. prohibiting peaceful assembly.
   D. restraining the reciting of prayers in public schools.

4. Judge Drago had to balance two rights that seemed to be competing for constitutional protection: _____
   A. the right to exercise the individual's religious preference versus the right of individuals not to have to experience the government's establishment of religion.
   B. the right to freedom of press versus the right to a fair trial.
   C. the right to be protected against stalking versus the state's right to protect against crime.
   D. the right to pray versus the right not to be subjected to school-sponsored prayers.

5. When legislators in Texas passed anti-stalking legislation, they tried to create legislation that did not violate the Constitutional guarantee to _____
   A. freedom of religion.
   B. freedom of speech.
   C. freedom of press.
   D. freedom of assembly.

6. According to the interpretation of the ACLU, the establishment clause of the First Amendment prohibits government _____
   A. prior restraint of the press.
   B. prosecution for religious beliefs.
   C. censorship of a religious activity.
   D. the use of public facilities to sponsor religious activities.

## TRUE/FALSE

If the statement is true, write "T" to the left of the statement. If the statement (or any part of the statement) is false, write "F" to the left of the statement.

7.  State legislatures may constitutionally pass laws that deny individuals the right to burn the flag in public.

8.  Because of religious convictions, parents can refuse to have their children vaccinated against smallpox even if the public welfare is seriously threatened.

## ESSAY PROBLEM QUESTIONS

9.  Explain why the federal court declared a "voluntary" school prayer as unconstitutional.

10. List those occasions where speech and press are not protected by the First Amendment.

11. What constitutional guidelines did legislators in Texas seek to follow in passing new anti-stalking legislation?

12. Discuss the difference between the establishment clause and the free exercise clause. How might they be in conflict? What position do the attorneys for the ACLU and the Legal Liberty Institute take?

# ANSWER KEY

The following provides the answers and references for the Practice Test questions.
Objectives are referenced using the following abbreviations:

T=Textbook Objectives   V=Video Objectives

| | Answer | Learning Objectives | References |
|---|---|---|---|
| 1. | C | T 2 | Kraemer, p. 318 |
| 2. | B | T1, V6 | Kraemer, p. 315, Video |
| 3. | B | V7 | Video |
| 4. | B | V8 | Video |
| 5. | B | V9 | Video |
| 6. | D | V10 | Video |
| 7. | F | T 1 | Kraemer, pp. 316–317 |
| 8. | F | T 3 | Kraemer, p. 320 |
| 9. | | T 5 | Kraemer, pp. 319–320 |
| 10. | | V6, V7 | Video |
| 11. | | V9 | Video |
| 12. | | V10 | Video |

# Lesson 25

# Rights of the Accused

## LESSON ASSIGNMENTS

Review the following assignments in order to schedule your time appropriately. For each lesson you will have a reading assignment and a video assignment.

Text:
> Kraemer, et al., *Texas Politics*, Chapter 10, "The Judiciary," pp. 331–335.

Video:
> "Rights of the Accused" from the series *Texas Politics and You*.

Activities:
> One or more activities may be assigned to this lesson. Refer to your syllabus.

## OVERVIEW

The procedural side of due process—establishing rights of the accused—was applied to the states slowly. Under our federal system, the administration of criminal justice had always been one of the responsibilities of the state governments. Therefore, the Supreme Court allowed the states to exercise their own criminal procedures and laws as long as they did not violate "fundamental principles of fairness."

But the question of fairness varied from state to state. Cases went before the Supreme Court to determine more exactly what restraints society must observe to be consistent with the federal Constitution. For example, the Sixth Amendment guarantees the accused "the assistance of counsel for his defense." Taken literally, this amendment does not say that counsel is mandatory in all cases nor does it say that the government has any obligation to appoint an attorney to ensure proper defense. Certain safeguards were outlined by the Supreme Court to guarantee that the principles in the Constitution are observed.

Most of the criminal procedure guarantees of the Bill of Rights—the Fourth, Fifth, Sixth, Seventh and Eighth Amendments in particular—were eventually incorporated into the due process clause of the Fourteenth Amendment as specific limitations on the state by the Warren Court in the 1960s. In our federal system, states are obliged to follow the U.S. Constitution and Supreme Court decisions; however, states can go further and offer more protection for the rights of the individual.

## LESSON GOAL

You should be able to understand the meaning and judicial interpretation of constitutional provisions dealing with due process of law and the rights of the accused.

## TEXTBOOK OBJECTIVES

The following objectives are designed to help you get the most from the text. Review them before reading the assignment. You may want to write notes to reinforce what you have learned.

1.  Explain how poor people are at a disadvantage when they are the accused in the criminal system in Texas.

2.  Describe and assess how legal assistance is provided for indigents.

3.  Explain the case of David Wayne Spence and its significance.

## VIDEO OBJECTIVES

The following objectives are designed to help you get the most from the video segment of this lesson. Review them before watching the video. You may want to write notes to reinforce what you have learned.

4.  Explain what is meant by "due process."

5. Describe the case of Brandon Hueber, and assess whether his case constitutes a violation of due process rights.

6. Discuss the role of the Texas Court of Criminal Appeals and the significance it had for Clarence Brandley and Susi Mobray.

7. Explain the significance of the Supreme Court's decision in the Clarence Earl Gideon case, and assess the steps that Texas takes to comply with the decision.

PRACTICE TEST

After reading the assignment, watching the video, and addressing the objectives, you should be able to complete the following Practice Test. Some essay questions in this Practice Test may be included in your exams. When you have completed the Practice Test, turn to the Answer Key to score your answers.

MULTIPLE CHOICE

Select the single best answer. If more than one answer is required, it will be so indicated.

1. Due process is a broad concept that _____
   A. allows people to be arrested and confined in order for society at large to be protected.
   B. allows the government the necessary discretion to make laws for the health, safety, and welfare of its citizens.
   C. establishes a general standard of fairness so that the rights of all citizens are impartially protected.
   D. all of the above.

2. The legislators who wrote the education law that affected Brandon Hueber were concerned with protecting _____
   A. the rights of school officials to run their educational system.
   B. due process for students before any educational benefits could be denied to them.
   C. all of the students to ensure a safe environment.
   D. both B and C.

3. The conviction and death sentence of Clarence Brandley was reversed by the Texas Court of Criminal Appeals because they found that there was a _____
   A. minor technicality.
   B. violation of due process.
   C. discovery that the prosecution focused on him solely because he was black and ignored other evidence that was inconsistent with Mr. Brandley's guilt.
   D. both B and C.

4. The Supreme Court decision in the Clarence Earl Gideon case held that if a person is too poor to hire an attorney, the Constitution _____
   A. requires the government to provide assistance for defense.
   B. requires that person to defend himself/herself.
   C. does not guarantee anyone the right to have an attorney.
   D. requires the government to provide assistance only in cases where the death penalty is relevant.

5. According to Judge Faith Johnson, her court-appointed attorneys are usually
   _____
   A. recent graduates from law school.
   B. law-school students.
   C. attorneys with at least three years of experience in criminal law.
   D. wealthy civil attorneys.

TRUE/FALSE

If the statement is true, write "T" to the left of the statement. If the statement (or any part of the statement) is false, write "F" to the left of the statement.

6. The judicial system in Texas is so simplified that anyone could easily defend himself or herself.

7. Murder suspects represented by court-appointed attorneys are more likely to be sentenced to death than are defendants with private counsel.

8. Texas has had an exceptional judicial history that illustrates that innocent people have never been placed on death row.

## ESSAY PROBLEM QUESTIONS

9. Describe the violation of proper procedures that occurred in the conviction of David Wayne Spence. How could these violations have been avoided? Why is this case especially disturbing?

10. Describe various ways the Constitution, the courts, and Texas protect the rights of persons accused of crimes.

11. Respond to the criticism that the appeals process is too technical and too costly.

## ANSWER KEY

The following provides the answers and references for the Practice Test questions. Objectives are referenced using the following abbreviations:

T=Textbook Objectives   V=Video Objectives

| | Answer | Learning Objectives | References |
|---|---|---|---|
| 1. | C | V4 | Video |
| 2. | D | V5 | Video |
| 3. | D | V6 | Video |
| 4. | A | V7 | Video |
| 5. | C | V7 | Video |
| 6. | F | T1 | Kraemer, p. 331 |
| 7. | T | T2 | Kraemer, p. 334 |
| 8. | F | T3 | Kraemer, pp. 332–335 |
| 9. | | T2, T3 | Video |
| 10. | | V4, V5, V6, V7 | Video |
| 11. | | V6, V7 | Video |

# Lesson 26

# Civil Rights and Equal Protection

## LESSON ASSIGNMENTS

Review the following assignments in order to schedule your time appropriately. For each lesson you will have a reading assignment and a video assignment.

Text:

Kraemer, et al., *Texas Politics*, Chapter 5, "Campaigns and Elections," pp. 129–136 and Chapter 11, "The Substance of Justice," pp. 325–331.

Video:

"Civil Rights and Equal Protection" from the series *Texas Politics and You*.

Activities:

One or more activities may be assigned to this lesson. Refer to your syllabus.

## OVERVIEW

Equality is rooted in the Declaration of Independence and is one of the ideals of American democracy, but it took a series of constitutional amendments and statutes to ensure that all U.S. citizens are treated equally under the law. A major source for protection against discrimination has been the Fourteenth Amendment to the U.S. Constitution which prohibits the states from denying "to any person within its jurisdiction" the equal protection of laws. Court decisions and congressional legislation, based on the Fourteenth Amendment and other provisions in the Constitution such as the power to regulate commerce, eventually removed barriers which denied the most basic human rights. While the concept of civil rights began with the struggle for equality by African Americans, other minorities have joined the cause.

## LESSON GOAL

You should be able to describe legal actions that have been taken and can be taken to protect the civil rights of people and to assure nondiscrimination and equality.

## TEXTBOOK OBJECTIVES

The following objectives are designed to help you get the most from the text. Review them before reading the assignment. You may want to write notes to reinforce what you have learned.

1.  Explain how civil rights differs from civil liberties.

2.  Describe how voting rights were extended to all citizens in Texas.

3.  Explain how the Fourteenth Amendment applies to public schools that are segregated on the basis of race.

4.  Explain how the problem of de facto segregation by economic class has resulted in educational inequality.

5.  Explain the significance of the Texas Supreme Court's ruling in *Edgewood Independent School District v. Kirby*.

## VIDEO OBJECTIVES

The following objectives are designed to help you get the most from the video segment of this lesson. Review them before watching the video. You may want to write notes to reinforce what you have learned.

6.  Define *civil rights* and explain the significance of the Fourteenth Amendment.

7.  Discuss how African Americans in Texas have struggled for civil rights.

8.  Describe what the Americans with Disabilities Act is designed to do.

9.  Explain the purpose of affirmative action, and evaluate the *Hopwood* decision and its impact beyond the University of Texas School of Law.

10. Explain how rights for women are protected in Texas, and assess the impact on women in the workplace.

PRACTICE TEST

After reading the assignment, watching the video, and addressing the objectives, you should be able to complete the following Practice Test. Some essay questions in this Practice Test may be included in your exams. When you have completed the Practice Test, turn to the Answer Key to score your answers.

MULTIPLE CHOICE

Select the single best answer. If more than one answer is required, it will be so indicated.

1. In the case of _____, a federal court declared the system of voter registration used in Texas to be unconstitutional.
   A. *Edgewood Independent School District v. Kirby*
   B. *Brown v. Board of Education*
   C. *Smith v. Allwright*
   D. *Beare v. Smith*
   E. none of the above

2. The "equal protection of the laws" clause, which was the basis of the Supreme Court's 1954 ruling declaring racial segregation in public school unconstitutional, is part of the _____ Amendment.
   A. First
   B. Fifth
   C. Tenth
   D. Fourteenth
   E. Sixteenth

3. In the case of _____, a state district court judge declared that the system of public education financing in Texas violated the state's constitution.
   A. *Edgewood Independent School District v. Kirby*
   B. *Brown v. Board of Education*
   C. *Smith v. Allwright*
   D. *Beare v. Smith*
   E. none of the above

4. "Civil rights" are basic human rights that include _____
   A. the right to vote, to get an education, and to get a job.
   B. the right to choose where to live.
   C. the right to be treated based on individual merits and not be denied because of a group identity.
   D. all of the above.

5. The Fourteenth Amendment _____
   A. prohibits states from denying any person within its jurisdiction the equal protection of the law.
   B. justifies the Supreme Court striking down segregation laws.
   C. justifies Congress in passing legislation that makes it a federal crime to prevent a citizen from voting.
   D. all of the above.

6. Grassroots activism by African Americans in Texas reflected a struggle to _____
   A. desegregate only businesses.
   B. obtain only the right to vote.
   C. obtain equal access to schools, jobs, and public places.
   D. create a separate school for whites and a separate but equal facility for blacks.

7. The goal of the Americans with Disabilities Act is to _____
   A. increase federal money for research into the development of advanced technology for artificial legs and arms.
   B. achieve accessible systems for people in wheelchairs and other mobility impaired individuals.
   C. ensure equal opportunities for those who are disabled.
   D. both B and C.

8. The purpose of affirmative action is to _____
   A. provide greater equality for minority groups.
   B. make a more inclusive society.
   C. give a preference to members of a particular group as a means of overcoming the consequences of past discrimination.
   D. all of the above.

9. The *Hopwood* decision _____
   A. struck down race-based affirmative action admission policies at the University of Texas School of Law as discriminatory against whites.
   B. upheld race-based affirmative action policies in state universities.
   C. abolished all affirmative action policies in city contracting with minorities.
   D. upheld all affirmative action policies in city contracting with minorities.

10. As a result of the 1997 "10 percent" Texas law written in response to the *Hopwood* decision, _____
    A. Texas public universities must automatically admit the students who graduate in the top 10 percent of their high schools.
    B. Texas public universities must recruit students from minority schools only.
    C. Texas public universities will accept only the top 10 percent of the students who have passed the standardized admissions test.
    D. Texas public universities must recruit 10 percent of their students from minority schools.

11. Women in the state of Texas have gained protection for their civil rights through _____
    A. the Texas Equal Rights Amendment.
    B. state legislation that eliminates sex-biased legal rights such as eliminating the right of a husband to rape his wife.
    C. Title IX of congressional legislation that was aimed at eliminating discrimination in education on the basis of sex.
    D. all of the above.

TRUE/FALSE

If the statement is true, write "T" to the left of the statement. If the statement (or any part of the statement) is false, write "F" to the left of the statement.

12. Civil rights refers to those actions that government must take to ensure equal treatment for everyone.


ESSAY PROBLEM QUESTIONS

13. How would you characterize the role played by Texas in the movement to extend civil rights in the United States? How has the state responded to federal court rulings pertaining to voting rights and school segregation?

14. Do you agree or disagree with the following statement: "All citizens are entitled to fair and equal treatment by government, even though that sometimes requires that individuals be treated differently"? Use specific amendments, court decisions, and laws to explain your answer.

15. What actions have been taken to establish rights and programs for the disabled?

16. Explain the *Hopwood* decision and the interpretation taken by Attorney General Morales, and assess the impact this may have on the goal of having a diverse student population.

17. What actions have been taken to advance the cause of equal rights for women?

# ANSWER KEY

The following provides the answers and references for the Practice Test questions. Objectives are referenced using the following abbreviations:

T=Textbook Objectives   V=Video Objectives

| | Answer | Learning Objectives | References |
|---|---|---|---|
| 1. | D | T2 | Kraemer, pp. 131–132 |
| 2. | D | T3 | Kraemer, pp. 325–326 |
| 3. | A | T5 | Kraemer, p. 326 |
| 4. | D | V6 | Video |
| 5. | D | V6 | Video |
| 6. | C | V7 | Video |
| 7. | D | V8 | Video |
| 8. | D | V9 | Video |
| 9. | A | V9 | Video |
| 10. | A | V9 | Video |
| 11. | D | V10 | Video |
| 12. | T | T1 | Kraemer, pp. 325–328 |
| 13. | | T1–T5 | Kraemer, pp. 325–332 |
| 14. | | V6–V10 | Video |
| 15. | | V8 | Video |
| 16. | | V9 | Video |
| 17. | | V1 | Video |

# Contributors

We gratefully acknowledge the valuable contributions to this course from the following individuals. The titles listed were accurate when the video programs were recorded, but may have changed since the original taping.

## LESSON 1—"TEXAS: WHO WE ARE"

*Frances Christian*, West Texas rancher, Claude, TX
*Tom Christian,* Son of West Texas rancher, Claude, TX
*Steve Murdock, Ph.D.*, Author, *Texas Challenged*; Department of Rural Sociology, Texas A&M University, College Station, TX
*Kim Ogden*, Director of Examinations and Assistant Director of the agency, Immigration and Naturalization Services, Dallas, TX
*Alvaro Piedrahita, Ana Maria Gomez-Piedrahita, Lucas Piedrahita*, new U.S. citizens, Dallas, TX
*Luis Plascencia*, Associate Director, The Tomas Rivera Policy Institute, Austin, TX
*Mary Sapp*, Executive Director, Texas Department on Aging, Austin, TX
*Carlos F. Truan,* Democrat; State Senator, District 20, Corpus Christi, TX
*Randy C. Wright*, Pharmacist, Claude Pharmacy, Claude, TX

## LESSON 2—"THE TEXAS CONSTITUTION"

*Dr. William Cunningham*, Chancellor, University of Texas System, Austin, TX
*Thomas Doebner*, Director of Funds Management, Texas Department of Transportation, Austin, TX
*Antonio O. Garza Jr.,* Secretary of the State of Texas, Austin, TX
*Donald R. Haragan*, President, Texas Tech University, Lubbock, TX
*Steve Levine*, Communications Director, Texas Lottery Commission, Austin, TX
*John Montford*, Former state senator; Chancellor, Texas Tech University and Texas Tech Medical Center, Lubbock, TX
*Laurence Olsen*, Executive Vice President, Texas Good Roads and Transportation Association, Austin, TX
*Michael Weiss*, Adjunct Professor, University of Houston, Houston, TX

## LESSON 3—"THE POLITICS OF THE ENVIRONMENT"

*Barbara Balderama*, Bilingual teacher, Socorro ISD, El Paso, TX
*J. E. "Buster" Brown*, Republican; State Senator, District 17; Chairperson, Senate Committee on Natural Resources, Austin, TX
*Elke Cumming*, Program Manager, Water Works, El Paso, TX
*Beverly Gattis*, President, Serious Texans Against Nuclear Dumping (STAND), Amarillo, TX
*Jesse W. Jones,* Democrat; State Representative, District 110, Dallas, TX
*Ken Kramer*, Director, Sierra Club Lone Star Chapter, Austin, TX
*Barry McBee*, Chairman, Texas Natural Resource Conservation Commission, Austin, TX
*Ricky Odom*, County Commissioner, Newton County, Deweyville, TX
*Maurice Osborn,* Mayor, City of Midlothian, Midlothian, TX
*Craig Pederson*, Executive Administrator, Texas Water Development Board, Austin, TX
*Judy Richards*, Duncanville City Council Member, Duncanville, TX
*Kel Seliger*, Mayor, City of Amarillo, Amarillo, TX
*Phillip and Doris Smith*, Panhandle Area Neighbors and Landowners, Panhandle, TX
*Deirdre Tinker*, Co-chairperson, Downwinders at Risk Fund, De Soto, TX
*Carlos F. Truan,* Democrat; State Senator, District 20, Corpus Christi, TX
*Peggy Venable*, Director, Texas Citizens for a Sound Economy, Austin, TX
*Tom Walton*, Director, Public Affairs, U.S. Department of Energy, Amarillo, TX
*David Waxman*, Consultant, Deep East Texas Council of Governments, Jasper, TX

## LESSON 4—"FEDERALISM AND TEXAS"

*Pat Carlson*, Member, Texas Eagle Forum, Grapevine, TX
*Diane Carroll*, Single parent with no insurance for children, Arlington, TX
*Roy Coffee*, Austin Director, Office of State and Federal Relations, Austin, TX
*Michael Cox*, Chief of Media Relations, Texas Department of Public Safety, Austin, TX
*Tom DeLay,* Republican; Member U.S. House of Representatives from Texas, Washington, DC
*Toby Goodman,* Republican; Member U.S. House of Representatives from Texas, Arlington, TX

*Kay Granger,* Republican; Member U.S. House of Representatives from Texas, Washington, DC

*Tyrette Hamilton,* Acting Executive Director, Texas Healthy Kids Corporation, Austin, TX

*Edward J. Harpham, Ph.D.,* Professor of Government and Political Economy, University of Texas at Dallas, Richardson, TX

*Angela Marshall,* Renaissance Neighborhood Advisory Panel, Renaissance Housing Program, Dallas, TX

*Jim Mattox,* Former Attorney General, 1983–1991, State of Texas, Austin, TX

*Mike McKinney,* Commissioner, Texas Health and Human Services Commission, Austin, TX

*Max Sandlin,* Democrat; Member U.S. House of Representatives from Texas, Washington, DC

*Bryan Sperry,* President, Children's Hospital Association of Texas, Austin, TX

*Mark W. Stiles,* Democrat; State Representative, District 21; Chairman, Calendars Committee, Beaumont, TX

*Bill Stinson,* Vice President of Governmental Affairs, Texas Association of Realtors, Austin, TX

*Leticia Van de Putte,* Democrat; State Representative, District 115, San Antonio, TX

*Mary K. Vaughn,* Director, City of Dallas Housing Department, Dallas, TX

*David Vela,* Director, Child Support Division, Office of Attorney General, State of Texas, Austin, TX

*Dianna Willis,* Single parent collecting back child support, Grand Prairie, TX


## LESSON 5—"LOCAL GOVERNMENTS IN TEXAS"

*Sue Bauman,* Vice President, Marketing and Communications, Dallas Area Rapid Transit, Dallas, TX

*William P. Burke,* Senior Vice President of Human Resources, Cadbury Beverages of America, Dallas, TX

*Rita and Tom Cox,* Urban family, Dallas, TX

*Mike Eastland,* Executive Director, North Texas Council of Governments, Dallas, TX

*Ron Kirk,* Mayor, City of Dallas, Dallas, TX

*R. Jan LeCroy,* President, Dallas Citizen's Council, Dallas, TX

*Michael Marcotte,* Director of Economic Development, City of Dallas, Dallas, TX

*Cole Morvan,* Executive Director of Economic Development, City of Plano, Plano, TX

*Mary Poss,* Mayor Pro Tem, North Texas Council of Governments, Dallas, TX

*David Rusk*, Author and urban expert, *Cities Without Suburbs*, Washington, DC

*Heywood Sanders*, Professor, Urban Administration, Trinity University, San Antonio, TX

*Norma Stanton*, Vice Chairman of the Board, Representative from Irving, Dallas Area Rapid Transit, Irving, TX

*William and Missy Turley*, Suburban family, Frisco, TX

*John Ware,* City Manager, City of Dallas, Dallas, TX

*Don Williams*, Chairman, Trammel Crow Company, Dallas, TX


## LESSON 6—"POLITICAL CULTURE"

*Russell Busby,* Attorney, President, Comfort Chamber of Commerce, Comfort, TX

*Manuel and Rosa Flores,* Activists in Corpus Christi, Corpus Christi, TX

*L. Tucker Gibson Jr.,* Chair and Professor of Political Science, Trinity University, San Antonio, TX

*Claudine Goree,* Seventh generation East Texan, Carthage, TX

*Gregory Krauter,* Director, Comfort Heritage Foundation, Comfort, TX

*Duane Parker,* Attorney, Third generation East Texan, Carthage, TX

*Bill and Marjorie Walraven,* Historians and journalists, Corpus Christi, TX


## LESSON 7—"COMMUNITY INVOLVEMENT"

*Caren Blackman*, Client, Family Pathfinders, Austin, TX

*Tillie Burgin*, Director, Mission Arlington/Mission Metroplex, Arlington, TX

*Alice Chapman*, Volunteer Coordinator, Mission Arlington/Mission Metroplex, Arlington, TX

*James Fishkin*, Professor of Government, University of Texas at Austin, Austin, TX

*Reverend David Garcia*, Rector, San Fernando Cathedral, Communities Organized for Public Service, San Antonio, TX

*Yesica Garcia*, Student, Terlingua High School, Terlingua, TX

*Dolores H. Hillyer*, Sponsor, Family Pathfinders, Austin, TX

*Kathy Killingsworth*, Superintendent, Terlingua County School District, Terlingua, TX

*Elzie Odom*, Mayor, City of Arlington, Arlington, TX

*Pat Ozuna*, Director, Communities Organized for Public Service, San Antonio, TX

*Jacqueline Pleasants*, Sponsor, Family Pathfinders, Austin, TX

*Ruthie Rainey*, Owner, Big Bend Motor Inn, Terlingua, TX

*Cynthia Scott*, Project Quest graduate, Communities Organized for Public Service, San Antonio, TX

*Reverend David Semrad*, Co-chair, Metro Alliance, Austin, TX

*John Sharp,* Comptroller of Public Accounts, State of Texas, Austin, TX

*Lucy Todd*, Director, Family Pathfinders, Austin, TX


## LESSON 8—"MEDIA AND PUBLIC AGENDA"

*Christopher F. Barbee*, Managing Editor, *El Campo Leader-News*, El Campo, TX

*Fred V. Barbee*, Publisher and Owner, *El Campo Leader-News*, El Campo, TX

*Lorelei Calvert*, Senior Vice President, General Manager, *Texas Monthly*, Austin, TX

*Cheryl Craigie*, President and CEO, KERA-TV, KDTN, North Texas Public Broadcasting, Incorporated, Dallas, TX

*Patti Diaz*, News Director, KPRR-FM, El Paso, TX

*Kay Granger,* Republican; Member U.S. House of Representatives from Texas, Washington, DC

*Molly Ivins*, Columnist, *Ft. Worth Star Telegram*, Austin, TX

*Ralph Langer*, Executive Vice President and Editor, *Dallas Morning News*, Dallas, TX

*Christopher Lee,* Journalist, *Dallas Morning News*, Dallas, TX

*John Miller*, Executive News Director, WFAA-TV, Dallas, TX

*Rebecca Muñoz-Diaz*, Vice President, General Market, KUVN-TV, Dallas, TX

*Paul Pugh*, Multimedia Director, *Texas Monthly*, Austin, TX

*Cat Simon*, Program Director, KTSM-AM, El Paso, TX

*Sylvester Turner,* Democrat; State Representative, District 139, Houston, TX

*Barry Vacker,* Assistant Professor, Center for Communication Arts, Southern Methodist University, Dallas, TX


## LESSON 9—"INTEREST GROUPS IN TEXAS"

*Thais Austin*, Government Affairs Director, Austin Board of Realtors, Austin, TX

*Robert Bryce*, Contributing Editor, *Austin Chronicle*, Austin, TX

*Helen Giddings,* Democrat; State Representative, District 109, De Soto, TX

*D. Brent Golemon*, President, Advanced Legal Technologies, Gallerywatch, Austin, TX

*Craig McDonald*, Director, Texans for Public Justice, Austin, TX

*Mike Moncrief,* Democrat; State Senator, District 12, Fort Worth, TX

*Atari Perry*, Member, Pearl Guards, Madison High School, Dallas, TX

*Ron Price*, Founder, Pearl Guards, Dallas, TX

*Belen Robles*, National President, League of United Latin American Citizens, Washington, DC

*Babe Schwartz*, Lobbyist and Former member of Texas legislature, Austin, TX

*Raymond Turner*, Member, Pearl Guards, Dallas, TX

*John Umphress*, Research Director, Public Citizen, Austin, TX

*Kenneth L. Young*, President, Pearl Guards, Dallas, TX

## LESSON 10—"POLITICAL PARTIES IN TEXAS"

*Nicole Broussard,* Field Director, Your Vote Your Voice, Dallas, TX

*Betty Brown,* Republican; State Representative Candidate, Terrell, TX

*Louis Davis*, President, Lake Highlands/White Rock Democrats, Dallas, TX

*Cheryl Demuro*, Student, Southern Methodist University, Dallas, TX

*Betty Doke*, Volunteer, Dallas County Council of Republican Women, Dallas, TX

*Bob Driegert*, Chairman, Dallas County Republican Party, Dallas, TX

*Takeesha Durgan*, Student, Southern Methodist University, Dallas, TX

*Mandy Goff*, Student, Southern Methodist University, Dallas, TX

*Lisa Hembry*, Candidate, U.S. Congressional District 30, Dallas, TX

*John Hendry*, Candidate, U.S. Congressional District 30, Dallas, TX

*Sue Hutchins*, President, Dallas County Council of Republican Women, Dallas, TX

*Eddie Bernice Johnson*, Democrat; Member U.S. House of Representative from Texas, Dallas, TX

*Jay Little*, Co-president, Southern Methodist University Democrats, Rockwall, TX

*Pat Mashburn*, Republican Party Delegate, Dallas, TX

*Keith Oakley,* Democrat; State Representative, District 4, Terrell, TX

*Tom Pauken*, State Chair, Republican Party of Texas, Dallas, TX

*Lisa Payne*, County Chair, Dallas County Democratic Party, Duncanville, TX

*Edward Sample*, Student, Southern Methodist University, Dallas, TX

*Dennis Simon*, Professor of Political Science, Southern Methodist University, Dallas, TX

*Watana Tucker*, Student, Southern Methodist University, Dallas, TX

*Martin Weiser*, Democratic Party Delegate, Dallas, TX

*Bill White*, State Chair, Democratic Party of Texas, Dallas, TX

*Charles Wynn*, College Republicans, Southern Methodist University, Dallas, TX

---

## LESSON 11—"THIRD PARTIES IN TEXAS"

*Mark Atkins*, Political Director, Texas Labor Party, Sanger, TX
*Sandra Bonsell*, Member, Natural Law Party, Austin, TX
*Howard Bridges Jr.*, Libertarian State Representative, District 110, Austin, TX
*Vicki Flores*, Dallas County Chair, Libertarian Party, Richardson, TX
*Jose Angel Gutierrez*, Founder, La Raza Unida, Dallas, TX
*Thomas Holmes*, Secretary, American Constitution Party of Texas, Fort Worth, TX
*Randal Morgan*, Libertarian Party Candidate, Texas Senate District 8, Dallas, TX
*Jim Riddlesperger*, Professor, Texas Christian University, Fort Worth, TX
*Ciro Rodriguez*, Democrat; Member U.S. House of Representatives, La Raza
   Unida, Dallas, TX
*Paul Truax*, Chairman, The Reform Party of Texas, Dallas, TX


## LESSON 12—"CAMPAIGNS AND ELECTIONS"

*Chuck Brandman*, School Board Candidate, CyFair Independent School District,
   Houston, TX
*Donna Ellis*, School Board Candidate, CyFair Independent School District,
   Cypress, TX
*Jeff Fisher*, Executive Director, Texas Christian Coalition, Fort Worth, TX
*Barbara Hines*, School Board Trustee, CyFair Independent School District,
   Cypress, TX
*Ron Kennedy*, School Board Candidate, CyFair Independent School District,
   Houston, TX
*Charlotte Lampe*, President, Families Organized for our Children's Unified School
   Year (FOCUS), Cypress, TX
*Scott Liebling*, School Board Candidate, CyFair Independent School District,
   Houston, TX
*Dolly Madison McKenna*, Liberty Tree, Houston, TX
*William O'Brien*, School Board Candidate, CyFair Independent School District,
   Cypress, TX
*Morris Overstreet*, Judge, Texas Court of Criminal Appeals, Austin, TX
*Rick Perry*, Commissioner, Texas Department of Agriculture, Austin, TX
*Marcus Powell*, School Board Candidate, CyFair Independent School District,
   Houston, TX

*Alan Quintero*, School Board Candidate, CyFair Independent School District, Cypress, TX

*Cecile Richards*, Executive Director, Texas Freedom Network, Austin, TX

*Karl Rove*, President, Karl Rove and Associates, Austin, TX

*Steven Salzar*, School Board Candidate, CyFair Independent School District, Houston, TX

*Rosie Sorells*, Member, Texas State Board of Education, Dallas, TX


## LESSON 13—"THE BALLOT BOX: VOTING UNDER TEXAS LAW"

*Mary Denny,* Republican; State Representative, District 63, Denton, TX

*Antonio O. Garza Jr.*, Secretary of the State of Texas, Austin, TX

*Franklin Jones*, Professor, Political Science, Texas Southern University, Houston, TX

*Nina Perales*, Staff Attorney, Mexican American Legal Defense and Educational Fund (MALDEF), San Antonio, TX

*John Wiley Price*, Dallas County Commissioner, City of Dallas, Dallas, TX

*Ann Richards*, Former Governor of Texas, 1991–1995, Austin, TX

*Belen Robles*, National President, League of United Latin American Citizens (LULAC), Washington, DC

*Bruce Sherbet*, Administrator, Dallas County Elections, Richardson, TX

*Jeanne Sommerfeld*, President, Texas National Organization for Women, Houston, TX

*John Stevens*, Chairperson, Political Action Committee, Gay and Lesbian Political Caucus, Dallas, TX

*Matan Wolfson*, Student, Project Vote class, Plano, TX

*Tessa and Martin Wolfson*, Parents, Plano, TX


## LESSON 14—"THE TEXAS LEGISLATURE"

*J. E. "Buster" Brown*, Republican; State Senator, District 17; Chairperson, Senate Committee on Natural Resources, Austin, TX

*Mike Ford*, Chairman, Texans for Initiative and Referendum, Austin, TX

*Kent Grusendorf,* Republican; State Representative, District 94, Arlington, TX

*William P. Hobby Jr.,* Democrat; Former Lieutenant Governor of Texas, 1973–1991, Houston, TX

*Pete Laney,* Democrat; Speaker of the House, Hale Center, TX

*Gib Lewis,* Democrat; Former Speaker of the House, Fort Worth, TX

*Jane Nelson,* Republican; State Senator, District 9, Flower Mound, TX
*Shirley Spellerberg,* Legislative Liaison, Texas Eagle Forum, Corinth, TX
*Mark W. Stiles,* Democrat; State Representative, District 21; Chairman, Calendars
    Committee, Beaumont, TX
*Carlos F. Truan,* Democrat; State Senator, District 20, Corpus Christi, TX
*Harvey Tucker,* Professor of Political Science, Texas A&M, College Station, TX
*Sylvester Turner,* Democrat; State Representative, District 139, Houston, TX
*Royce West,* Democrat; State Senator, District 23, Dallas, TX


LESSON 15—"THE LEGISLATIVE PROCESS IN TEXAS"

*Warren Chisum,* Republican; State Representative, District 88, Pampa, TX
*Jeff Fisher,* Executive Director, Texas Christian Coalition, Fort Worth, TX
*Alvin Granoff,* Former State Representative, 1983–1995, Dallas, TX
*Dianne Hardy-Garcia,* Executive Director, Lesbian/Gay Rights Lobby of Texas,
    Austin, TX
*John Heasely,* General Counsel, Texas Bankers Association, Austin, TX
*Mike Kelly,* Lobbyist, Campaign for Tobacco-Free Kids, Austin, TX
*Mike Moncrief,* Democrat; State Senator, District 12, Fort Worth, TX
*Jerry Patterson,* Republican; State Senator, District 11, Houston, TX
*John Sharp,* Comptroller of Public Accounts, State of Texas, Austin, TX
*Mark W. Stiles,* Democrat; State Representative, District 21; Chairman of
    Calendars Committee, Beaumont, TX
*Bill Stinson,* Vice President of Governmental Affairs, Texas Association of
    Realtors, Austin, TX
*Arlene Wohlgemuth,* Republican; State Representative, District 58, Burleson, TX
*Steven Wolens,* Democrat; State Representative, District 103, Dallas, TX
*Vivienne Armstrong and Louise Young,* Supporters of same-sex marriage, Dallas, TX


LESSON 16—"TEXAS: CASEWORK AND OVERSIGHT"

*Pete P. Gallego,* Democrat; State Representative, District 74, Alpine, TX
*Michael V. Johnson,* Detective, Plano Police Department, Plano, TX
*James Oberwetter,* Chairman, Texas Commission on Alcohol and Drug Abuse,
    Dallas, TX
*Jerry Patterson,* Republican; State Senator, District 11, Houston, TX

*Florence Shapiro,* Republican; State Senator, District 8, Dallas, TX

*Beverly Woolley*, Republican; State Representative, District 136, Houston, TX


## LESSON 17—"THE GOVERNOR"

*George W. Bush,*  Governor, State of Texas, Austin, TX

*David Cain*, Democrat; State Senator, District 2, Dallas, TX

*William P. Clements Jr.*, Former Governor of Texas, 1979–1983, 1987–1991, Dallas, TX

*William McKenzie*, Associate Editorial Page Editor, *Dallas Morning News*, Dallas, TX

*Ann Richards,* Former Governor of Texas, 1991–1995, Austin, TX

*Clay Robison,* Journalist, *Houston Chronicle*, Austin, TX

*Karl Rove*, President, Karl Rove and Associates, Austin, TX

*Vicki Spriggs*, Executive Director, Texas Juvenile Probation Commission, Austin, TX


## LESSON 18—"TEXAS BUREAUCRACY"

*Michael Jones*, Public Information Director, Texas Department of Human Services, Austin, TX

*Camille Keith*, Vice President, Special Marketing, Southwest Airlines; Nursing Home Reform Advocate, Dallas, TX

*Joey Longley*, Director, Sunset Advisory Commission, Austin, TX

*Michael McKinney*, Commissioner, Texas Health and Human Services Commission, Austin, TX

*Elliott Naishtat*, Democrat; State Representative, District 49, Austin, TX

*Debra F. Owens*, Director, Texas Diabetes Council/Texas Department of Health, Austin TX

*John Sharp,* Comptroller of Public Accounts, State of Texas, Austin, TX

*Tom Smith*, Director, Public Citizen, Austin, TX

*Tammy Spencer*, Lone Star Card user, Austin, TX

*Melissa Todd*, Division Chairperson, Elder Law and Public Health, Office of the Attorney General, Austin, TX

*Martha Whitehead*, Former State Treasurer of Texas, Tyler, TX

## LESSON 19—"FISCAL POLICY"

*Fred Ashworth*, Sheriff, Newton County, Orange, TX

*Norman Baxter*, Superintendent, Sunnyvale Independent School District, Sunnyvale, TX

*David Cain,* Democrat; State Senator, District 2, Dallas, TX

*Tom Craddick*, Republican; State Representative, District 82; Chairman, Committee on Ways and Means, Midland, TX

*Stephen and Allie Ku*, Upper-income family, Plano, TX

*Dick Lavine*, Fiscal Analyst, Center for Public Policy Priorities, Austin, TX

*Charldean Newell*, Regents Professor of Public Administration, University of North Texas, Denton, TX

*Bill Ratliff,* Republican; State Senator, District 1; Chairman, Senate Finance Committee, Mt. Pleasant, TX

*Ella and Brent Romney*, Middle-income family, Dallas, TX


## LESSON 20—"GLOBALISM: NAFTA AND TEXAS"

*Brenda Arnett*, Director, Texas Department of Economic Development, Austin, TX

*Norma Bueno*, TAA/NAFTA Supervisor, Texas Workforce Commission, El Paso, TX

*Jaime Campos*, Human Resources Manager, First Alert, El Paso, TX

*Diane Feffer*, Director of International Marketing, Cinemark International, Dallas, TX

*Rosie Guerrero*, Instructor, Automated Office Skills, Center for Employment Training, El Paso, TX

*Donald A. Hicks*, Professor of Political Economy, University of Texas at Dallas, Richardson, TX

*Ken Higgins*, Vice President, Cinemark International, Dallas, TX

*Jose E. Martinez*, President and CEO, Free Trade Alliance, San Antonio, TX

*Eric Myers*, Communications Director, Coalition for Justice in the Maquiladoras, Kennett Square, PA

*Diana Natalicio*, President, University of Texas at El Paso, El Paso, TX

*Arnulfo Porras*, Truck driver, NAFTA retraining program, El Paso, TX

*Ed Sills*, Communications Director, Texas AFL-CIO, Austin, TX

*Lori L. Taylor*, Senior Economist and Policy Advisor, Federal Reserve Bank of Dallas, Dallas, TX

*Tom Thomas*, Senior Vice President, Economic Development, El Paso Greater Chamber of Commerce, El Paso, TX

# LESSON 21—"THE TEXAS COURTS AND THE CRIMINAL JUSTICE SYSTEM"

*Patsy Day*, Executive Director, Victim's Outreach, Dallas, TX

*Tony Fabelo*, Executive Director, Criminal Justice Policy Council, Austin, TX

*Vicki Hallman*, Assistant Regional Director, Texas Department of Criminal Justice Parole Division, Dallas, TX

*Faith Johnson*, Judge, Criminal District Court 363, Dallas County, De Soto, TX

*Linda Marin*, Executive Director, Texas CURE, Austin, TX

*Mike Morrow*, Superintendent, Windham School District, Huntsville, TX

*Allan Polunsky*, Chairman, Texas Board of Criminal Justice, San Antonio, TX

*Wayne Scott*, Executive Director, Texas Department of Criminal Justice Institutional Division, Huntsville, TX

*John Sharp,* Comptroller of Public Accounts, State of Texas, Austin, TX

*M. B. Thaler*, Senior Warden, Texas Department of Criminal Justice Institutional Division, Huntsville, TX


# LESSON 22—"JUDICIAL SELECTION IN TEXAS"

*Greg Abbott*, Judge, Texas Supreme Court, Austin, TX

*Roberto Alonzo,* President, Mexican American Democrats of Texas, Dallas, TX

*Diana Clark*, Volunteer, League of Women Voters, Dallas, TX

*Bob Gammage*, Retired Judge, Texas Supreme Court, Llano, TX

*James Harrington*, Legal Director, Texas Civil Rights Project, Austin, TX

*Clay Johnson*, Appointment Director, Office of Governor Bush, Dallas, TX

*Tom Luce*, Partner and Chairperson, Judicial Selection Task Force, Luce and Williams, Dallas, TX

*Frank Maloney*, Judge, Texas Court of Criminal Appeals, Austin, TX

*Jesse Oliver*, Former Judge, 95th Judicial District Court, Dallas, TX

*Tom Price*, Judge, Texas Court of Criminal Appeals, Austin, TX

*Martin E. Richter*, Criminal District Judge, 116th District Court, Dallas, TX

*Rose Spector*, Trial Judge, Texas Supreme Court, Austin, TX

## LESSON 23—"DECISION MAKING BY THE COURTS"

*Lee Alcorn,* President, Dallas National Association for the Advancement of
    Colored People, Dallas, TX
*William Conover III,* General Counsel, Texas Commission on Human Rights,
    Austin, TX
*Frances T. Farenthold,* Political Activist, Houston, TX
*Raul A. Gonzalez,* Judge, Texas Supreme Court, Austin, TX
*Anthony Griffin,* Attorney, Anthony Griffin, Incorporated, Galveston, TX
*James Harrington,* Legal Director, Texas Civil Rights Project, Austin, TX
*Jay Jacobson,* Executive Director, Texas American Civil Liberties Union, Austin, TX
*Sharon Keller,* Judge, Texas Court of Criminal Appeals, Austin, TX
*Dan McCrory,* Assistant District Attorney, Harris County District Attorney's
    Office, Spring, TX
*Mike Moncrief,* Democrat; State Senator, District 12, Fort Worth, TX
*Peggy Romberg,* Executive Director, Texas Family Planning Association, Austin, TX
*Stanley G. Schneider,* Attorney at Law, Schneider & McKinney L.P., Houston, TX

## LESSON 24—"FIRST AMENDMENT CIVIL LIBERTIES"

*Doug Adams,* President and General Manager, KXAS-TV, Fort Worth, TX
*Ron Bradford,* Superintendent, Elgin Independent School District, Elgin, TX
*Hattie Cole,* Stalking victim, Dallas, TX
*Joe Drago,* Judge, Criminal District Court #4, Fort Worth, TX
*Cindy Dyer,* Assistant District Attorney, Dallas County District Attorney's Office,
    Dallas, TX
*Brian McCall,* Republican; State Representative, District 66, Plano, TX
*Mike Moncrief,* Democrat; State Senator, District 12, Fort Worth, TX
*Diana Philip,* Regional Director, North Texas American Civil Liberties Union,
    Dallas, TX
*James Rogers,* Professor of Political Science, Texas A&M University, College
    Station, TX
*Kelly Schackleford,* Executive Director, Free Market Foundation, Allen, TX
*Mac Nabours, Tom and Kaye Stiles,* Establishment clause case, Austin, TX

# LESSON 25—"RIGHTS OF THE ACCUSED"

*Scottie D. Allen*, Attorney, Scottie D. Allen and Associates, Dallas, TX
*Charles Baird*, Judge, Texas Court of Criminal Appeals, Austin, TX
*J. E. "Buster" Brown*, Republican; State Senator, District 17; Chairperson, Senate
    Committee on Natural Resources, Austin, TX
*Scott Hochberg*, Democrat; State Representative, District 132, Houston, TX
*Barbara Hueber,* Plaintiff, Due process case, Arlington, TX
*Faith Johnson*, Judge, Criminal District Court 363, De Soto, TX
*Arch McColl*, Attorney, McColl and McColloch, Dallas, TX
*Jane Roden*, Chief Public Defender, Public Defender's Office, Dallas, TX
*Carrie Sperling*, Attorney for Brandon Hueber, Dallas, TX


# LESSON 26—"CIVIL RIGHTS AND EQUAL PROTECTION"

*Michael Greve*, Co-founder and Executive Director, The Center for Individual
    Rights, Washington, DC
*Lani Guinier*, Civil Rights Lawyer; Law Professor, University of Pennsylvania,
    Philadelphia, PA; Author, *The Tyranny of the Majority: Fundamental
    Fairness in Representative Democracy*, Washington, DC
*Arthur and Daisy Joe*, Directors, Black Citizens for Justice Law and Order, Dallas, TX
*Carmella Jones*, Sheriff, Armstrong County, Claude, TX
*Genice Rabe*, Attorney, Law Offices of A. G. Rabe, Dallas, TX
*Jeanne Sommerfeld*, President, Texas National Organization for Women, Houston, TX
*Kent Waldrep*, President and CEO, National Paralysis Foundation, Dallas, TX
*Royce West,* Democrat; State Senator, District 23, Dallas, TX
*Everitt Winters*, Director of Affirmative Action, Southern Methodist University,
    Dallas, TX